Critical Issues in Curriculum
John Willinksy, Series Editor

Powerful Writing, Responsible Teaching

TIMOTHY J. LENSMIRE

Teachers College, Columbia University
New York and London

Published by Teachers College Press, 1234 Amsterdam Avenue, New York, NY 10027

Library of Congress Cataloging-in-Publication Data

Lensmire, Timothy J., 1961–
   Powerful writing, responsible teaching / Timothy J. Lensmire.
      p. cm. — (Critical issues in curriculum series)
   Includes bibliographical references and index.
   ISBN 0-8077-3956-1 (pbk. : alk. paper) — ISBN 0-8077-3957-X (cloth : alk. paper)
      1. English language—Composition and exercises—Study and teaching.
   2. Critical pedagogy.   I. Title. II. Series.
   LB1576.L42   2000
   808'.042'071173—dc21   00-021070

ISBN 0-8077-3956-1 (paper)
ISBN 0-8077-3957-X (cloth)

Printed on acid-free paper
Manufactured in the United States of America

07 06 05 04 03 02 01 00   8 7 6 5 4 3 2 1

For Ruth

He came more and more to be unable to care for, or think of soul but as in an actual body, or of any world but that wherein are water and trees, and where men and women look, so or so, and press actual hands.

—Walter Pater

My point is not that everything is bad, but that everything is dangerous. If everything is dangerous, then we always have something to do.

—Michel Foucault

Yes, the chances of paradise are small. So what?

—Toni Morrison

Contents

Contents

Acknowledgments

Many have been generous with intellectual and emotional support as I worked on this book. Thank you to David Cohen, Gerald Early, Carole Edelsky, Brian Ellerbeck, Steve Griffin, Annette Henry, Deborah Hicks, David Jardine, Jay Lemke, John Jacob Lensmire, Sarah Lensmire, Janet Miller, Janet Navarro, Jeremy Price, Jane Ritger-Lensmire, Michael W. Smith, and Jim Swaim. Special thanks to James Garrison and John Willinsky for their ongoing support of my work.

My colleagues in the Department of Education at Washington University in St. Louis have created a stimulating place for me to learn and write. Thanks especially to Phyllis Balcerzak, Diane Beals, Garrett Duncan, Mary Ann Dzuback, Donna Gardner, James Wertsch, and the late Arthur Wirth. I also want to acknowledge the impact of the larger Washington University community, and its meanings and values, on my life and work: ting-a-ling.

Finally, my thanks to Matthew Cooper and Emmanuel Harris II. Their friendship has sustained me and is, perhaps, the strongest argument I have for the worthiness of sharing our stories and rehearsing new ways of being and acting in the world, together.

I gratefully acknowledge the support of the National Academy of Education and its Spencer Fellowship Program.

Introduction

My laugh is too big. The embarrassed faces of my university colleagues taught me this. At first I was confused, a little worried. I was a beginning assistant professor. What was I doing to alienate these potential friends who might sit and talk with me about wonderful, worthy things (these certain evaluators who would sit and judge me as worthy or not of the university)? Then I was hurt. I laugh loudest when (whack) the meaningfulness-ridiculousness of life is made plain. At exactly the moment I assumed, trusted, abandoned decorum for, lost my self to this obvious truth, I was rejected. The rejections were small, certainly. Momentary (still punishing).

I tried laughing smaller, softer, politely. Then I laughed louder on purpose, tried not to care—screw it.

It's a rural, small-town, northern Wisconsin laugh. My father's laugh.

When my dad retired—he was a cheesemaker for over 40 years in a small factory owned by local dairy farmers—my mom threw a party. She asked my brother Jeff and my sister Sue and me to say a few words. I didn't want to, because that sounded like a funeral. But I was wrong.

My brother developed a "B" theme as he re-membered summers he worked with Dad in the cheese factory: Jeff wore *Red Ball* brand rubber boots; he had to stay alert, stay on the *balls* of his feet; he sweated a lot (the factory was very hot and humid) so his . . . certain *body* parts itched, and he scratched them. Sue talked about how, when we were little, we had to get up before sunrise on Christmas Day (usually so cold) so we could go to church together, because back then my dad worked seven days a week, even on Christmas (cows gave milk every day). They spoke well, made people laugh, start crying.

They didn't have anything written down. I did, and I felt stupid. But then I decided that that's what I was, a writer—and I realized that this was the first time I would stand before these people, this community in which I grew up, as one. This is what I had written on a small piece of paper, what I read:

All of you know that my dad is a hard-working person. Now, as I've lived and moved around a little, I've met many hard-working people. Unfortunately, for many of these people, it seems that hard work shrivels up their spirit. Every extra hour of labor seems to cost them some of their kindness—every struggle they endure becomes a sign for them of their superiority, as if working hard gives them the right to sit in judgement of others. My dad does not live this way in the world. His life of hard work seems to make him more sympathetic to others' struggles, quicker to be generous with his family and friends and neighbors and strangers, who are, after all, also just doing the best that they can. I'm thankful to my dad for showing me how dignified hard work can be when it is joined to a generous, caring spirit.

I confess that I played the pedagogue, wagged my finger here, just a bit. This retirement party for my dad took place in December 1994, soon after the Republican Party's victory in Congress that year. I was sick of hearing a truly ungenerous rhetoric heralded as the voice of the people. Good, hard-working people stood before me—but I had heard more than a few of them practicing this rhetoric, trying on this hard-hearted talk (I don't think their hearts were hard, but maybe with practice). So I talked back. I don't think I overdid it. When I looked up from my reading, my aunts and uncles nodded, reassured that I had focused my attention where it should have been—on their brother, John, my dad—and captured something important about him.

*   *   *

If stories about the author in an academic book seem improper to you or make you nervous or bored, have no fear. This book is about writing in schools and radical democracy. In the chapters that follow, I sometimes invoke experiences that I have had in the classroom, but not until the Conclusion do I tell another personal story from my private life. (Consider yourself warned: that story is about, among other things, sex, the Catholic Church, and me. If you don't want to read it, then please don't.)

That said, this book is, in other ways, thoroughly and consistently personal. In chapter 1, "Writing Workshop as Carnival," I draw heavily on my own teaching and research in a third grade classroom. My goal in this chapter is to explore what sort of learning environment and classroom community writing workshops provide for students in schools. My method is to portray the workshop as a form of carnival.

When I say *writing workshop*, I mean the kind of primary and secondary school writing classes imagined, researched, popularized, and promoted by Donald Graves (1983, 1994), Lucy Calkins (1986, 1991), and Nancie Atwell (1987). In general, I think that writing workshop approaches have transformed teacher and student roles, writing tasks, and classroom organization in positive ways. I interpret workshops as sites of possibility, as offering opportunities for learning not found in traditional classrooms. Although others have certainly contributed to my understanding and images of what writing workshops are supposed to be like (e.g., Donald Murray, 1979, 1985), it is Graves, Calkins, and Atwell who have been most influential. When I point to *workshop advocates* in this book, I refer to these writers.

When I say *carnival*, I mean the kind of living that Russian literary theorist and philosopher Mikhail Bakhtin (1984a, 1984b) associated with the carnivals and popular festivals of the Middle Ages and Renaissance. Bakhtin thought that such social contexts could teach us much about how to bust open and transform traditional, restrictive spaces and talk. In chapter 1, I use the lessons of Bakhtin's carnival and my work with third graders both to affirm and question the workshop's guiding vision: children writing themselves and their worlds on the page, within a classroom setting that liberates student intention and association.

This book is personal, then, because it is profoundly shaped by my own experiences as an educator. It is also personal in the sense that I try, as best I can, to keep *persons*—living, growing selves, flesh-and-blood humans—before us, center stage, as I theorize the teaching and learning of writing in schools. Dell Hymes (1972) once complained that the study of language too often takes a "Garden of Eden" perspective in which the "controlling image is of an abstract, isolated individual, almost an unmotivated cognitive mechanism, not, except incidentally, a person in a social world" (p. 272). Unfortunately, workshop advocates imagine teachers and students similarly—imagine them as abstracted from the smaller and larger social contexts within which they move, as isolated from the complexity and conflict of human association and institution. Workshop advocates pretend we never ate the apple. And by embracing this Garden of Eden view, they simply ignore much of our own fallen world (our home), where "meanings may be won by the sweat of the brow, and communication is achieved in labor" (p. 272). They ignore much of the difficulty (and satisfaction), the struggle (and joy), of teaching and writing in schools.

In chapter 2, "Teacher as Dostoevskian Novelist," I examine teaching and the teacher's role in writing workshops. Bakhtin's (1984a) work is again important—this time, his celebratory reading of Fyodor Dostoevsky's fiction. For Bakhtin, Dostoevsky's novels featured strong characters who, in dialogue with each other and the author, articulate a plurality (a *polyphony*) of worldviews and truths. And this in sharp contrast to the *monologic* novels of most other writers—novels with a single worldview (that of the novelist) mouthed by servile characters. In this chapter, I look to Bakhtin's analysis of Dostoevsky in order to celebrate and criticize how workshop advocates have conceptualized teaching and the teacher. I do this with a metaphor: I imagine the teacher as a novelist—a Dostoevskian novelist—who creates a polyphonic classroom-novel and takes up dialogic relations with student characters. With this metaphor, I begin to revise the roles and responsibilities of workshop teachers.

I explore and reconstruct workshop images of students and their writing in chapter 3, "Voice as Project." Student voices have not fared well in our schools. Whether spoken or written, they have too often been reduced to lifeless, guarded responses—responses to the questions and assignments of powerful others, responses formed in the shadow of teacher scrutiny and evaluation. In this chapter, I describe how workshop advocates and others have conceived of student voice. Then, I propose an alternative conception that, I hope, has a better feel for how writing feels for students, one that better recognizes the dangers and possibilities of student expression in schools.

In the end, I grab hold of writing workshop approaches, shake them, break them, remake them, for one reason: I hope to help teachers and students live worthier lives in schools. And for me, *worthier* lives means *more democratic* lives.

I need to be as clear as I can here, since, in these ugly times, ugly things roam and reproduce under the cover of *democracy*. By democracy, I do not mean whatever form of capitalism the United States is currently selling to other countries. I do not mean more decisions made by markets (and, oh, could you educators please crank out more workers who think it is exciting to lose their jobs and benefits when it is profitable for stockholders?). I do not mean a grand cultural tradition preserved for us in the good old history textbooks (slaves were happy back then), virtuous children's stories (girls and women were happy back then), and the finest American literature (I don't know why all the authors are white men—hmmm, that's a puzzle).

I do not even mean, in the main, a very reasonable, worthy meaning of democracy—one to which public schools have paid some attention in the past, one for which we must struggle, one under attack by conservatives who want schools and the state to serve ever more efficiently the demands of capital, patriarchy, and white supremacy—democracy as political system, as form of government. I think that the sort of living I propose for students and teachers would make a powerful contribution to the education of future citizens, that it supports the development of capacities for thought, feeling, and action required if democratic institutions and procedures are to flourish. But the meaning of *democracy* (the goal for school writing) I pursue in this book is more immediate, present day, everyday. Humbler. Harder.

When I say *democracy*, I mean what John Dewey (1951) called a "way of life"—a way of life that is "controlled by a working faith in the possibilities of human nature" (p. 391). This working faith is not an intermittent, abstract faith in human possibility, one that works only on Sundays or when our eyes glaze over in satisfied contemplation of the progress of humankind. Instead, it is a working, workaday faith that guides and expresses itself in our everyday habits and interactions with others. It is a faith I continue to learn about from my dad, John, as I watch and experience how his generous, caring spirit moves in the world.

Dewey, writing in 1939, emphasized the personal aspects and demands of such a way of life and faith:

> To denounce Naziism for intolerance, cruelty and stimulation of hatred amounts to fostering insincerity if, in our personal relations to other persons, if in our daily walk and conversation, we are moved by racial, color, or other class prejudice; indeed, by anything save a generous belief in their possibilities as human beings, a belief which brings with it the need for providing conditions which will enable these capacities to reach fulfillment. (1951/1939, p. 391)

Dewey, of course, dedicated much of his life and writing to figuring out how education—and specifically education in schools—might provide conditions for the development of human capacity in all its diversity and power. In this essay, however, and in the larger context of the rise of fascism and Stalinism, Dewey (1951/1939) invoked not school but home and street corner as sites where democracy would live or die:

> When I think of the conditions under which men and women are living in many foreign countries today, fear of espionage, with danger hanging over the meeting of friends for friendly conversation in private gatherings, I am inclined to believe that the heart and final guarantee of democracy is in free gatherings of neighbors on the street corner to discuss back and forth what is read in uncensored news of the day, and in gatherings of friends in the living rooms of houses and apartments to converse freely with one another. (p. 392)

This is what I am shooting for, this meaning of democracy, this way of life. In schools. In classrooms that are *living* rooms gathering friends for intimate conversation, gathering neighbors from up and down the street (not just the gated village) to deliberate—sometimes softly, sometimes loudly, with and without heat—the stories of the day.

I focus on life inside classrooms, and I often write as if teachers and students get to make this life up as they please. Of course this is not true.

Indeed, the odds (I mean the status quo in school and society) are against students and teachers pulling off this democratic project in workshops. The odds improve if teachers' work is organized in ways that enable them to move with agency, responsibility, dignity in schools; if the meanings and values of students, parents, and communities are attended to in curriculum, evaluation, administration; if state and federal funding actually assures that all students and teachers have classrooms and schools (not falling down on their heads) with books, pens, paper (I know I am supposed to ask for computers, but even books, pens, paper would be nice); if public schools survive at all. There is much to do, much more not addressed in this book.

Still, even as schools and society are struggled over and change (for good and for bad), students and teachers make their way through all these days in classrooms, making up, living (even if not as they please) lives.

I conclude my effort to make up better lives in writing workshops, to reconstruct workshop approaches in a Deweyan image of democratic living, in chapter 4, "Community, Deliberation, and Transgressive Stories." This chapter is about stories. It is about helping students to imagine new roles and lives for themselves in our society: new because they don't like the old ones, new because the old ones won't work in a new world, new because they had no roles in the old stories (were supposed to be grateful just for the opportunity to sit in the auditorium and watch as others played the leads). I discuss how workshops might yet embrace the sort of rich, life-sustaining, and critical conversations called for by Dewey (1916/1966) in his *Democracy and Education*, analyzed and celebrated by Patricia Hill Collins (1991) in her *Black Feminist Thought*, and demonstrated by Richard Bernstein (1992) in his *The New Constellation*. I discuss how workshops might yet provide the conditions students need to experience and imagine new relations with others, envision and create new, humane, livable worlds.

*   *   *

I live in a similar and different world now from the one in which I grew up, where I learned to laugh. I am the same and different. I remain white, male, enjoy privileges in this society because of this, because of too many years of schooling. My friends and neighbors have changed. Early religious and moral commitments have become moral and political commitments to creative, radical democracy. These worlds, accidents, purposes, people, help and hinder what I understand, what I imagine, what I write. I am not an unmotivated cognitive mechanism. I am a person (I take a position) in a social world.

This position is not just my doing. I have been positioned by others in the past, by what they thought I should be because of my sex and skin color and where I came from. I have been positioned by others in the past who looked at me and imagined, generously, what I could become. You, gentle reader, position me now as you read what I write, as you respond to my attempts to position myself and this book.

Let me try one more.

I am driving down the street in a rusty white car with my son John and my daughter Sarah in the backseat. It's an early-summer St. Louis day, windows rolled down, radio very loud. I am joyful, a little nervous, because I am going to an outdoor basketball court where I haven't played before, which means that I will have to show a new group of people that I can hoop a little (maybe, way down, I'm a little joyful, a little nervous, because I will probably be the only white player there—but I am getting used to playing with my new neighbors and friends). Then an old Jethro Tull song comes on. But I have no idea it is by Jethro Tull (I guess instead some new alternative rock band because I hear an accordion). I have no idea it is an old song. It is stunning, exhilarating, seems perfect for this hot, humid day (even as its refrain stretches me back to the middle of winter, Wisconsin).

This is what I heard:

Do you ever get the feeling
that the story's too damn real
and in the present
tense?
Or that everybody's on the stage
and it seems like you're the only person
sitting in the audience?
Skating away
Skating away
Skating away, on the thin ice of a new day.

1

Writing Workshop as Carnival

This is a very important aspect of a carnival sense of the world. People who in life are separated by impenetrable hierarchical barriers enter into free familiar contact in the carnival square. . . . All *distance* between people is suspended.
— Mikhail Bakhtin, *Problems of Dostoevsky's Poetics*

Travel, economic and commercial tendencies, have at present gone far to break down external barriers; to bring peoples and classes into closer and more perceptible connection with one another. It remains for the most part to secure the intellectual and emotional significance of this physical annihilation of space.
— John Dewey, *Democracy and Education*

Mikhail Bakhtin (1984b) called carnival the "second life" of the people. He thought that the carnivals and popular festivals of the Middle Ages and Renaissance conferred the "right to emerge from the routine of life, the right to be free from all that is official and consecrated" (p. 257). This second life of the people was both unofficial and antiofficial— unofficial because the playful, fearless spirit of carnival loosened the grip of established norms and relations and allowed alternatives to emerge in their place; antiofficial because this same carnivalistic spirit engendered and supported the criticism and mockery of the official social order and ideology.

In this chapter, I compare writing workshops to Bakhtin's carnival and argue that workshops embody important carnival characteristics. Workshops create unofficial spaces in schools, loosen the grip of traditional roles and tasks in classrooms through increased student control of their own literate activities. These unofficial spaces, however, are not without their limitations and problems. Workshops, as currently imagined, are seldom antiofficial, and then only accidentally. And workshop advocates ignore how these unofficial spaces might support not only the expression of something new, but also the (sometimes violent) reassertion of old power relations, old meanings and values.

Many of the examples I use to evoke workshop life in this chapter are drawn from teacher research I first wrote about in *When Children Write* (Lensmire, 1994). In that book, my primary concern was to describe my own and my third grade students' experiences and activities in a particular writing workshop—our hopes; our relations; our struggles with teaching, learning, and writing. In this chapter, my subject is the critical examination of writing workshop approaches as an agenda for writing classrooms, as a blueprint for democratic living.

BAKHTIN ON CARNIVAL

I emphasize four features of Bakhtin's carnival.[1] The first is the *participation of all* in carnival. Carnival, for Bakhtin, is not a spectacle, not something performed by some and watched by others. Instead, the line between spectator and performer is blurred, as in the 18th-century Roman carnival described by Goethe (1970) in his *Italian Journey*. During carnival, participants move in and out of processions, games, mock battles with confetti, verbal duels, and exaggerated reenactments of the body's struggles with birth and death. For Bakhtin (1984b), it is only later, with the encroachment of the state on popular festive life and the movement of festive life from the marketplace to the private household, that the people's participation in carnival shifts toward spectatorship—carnival becomes a parade, and the carnival spirit is "transformed into a mere holiday mood" (p. 33). The full-bodied carnival that interests Bakhtin features an active, universal participation, is a "play without footlights" (p. 235): "Carnival is not contemplated and, strictly speaking, not even performed; its participants live in it, they live by its laws as long as those laws are in effect; that is, they live a carnivalistic life" (Bakhtin, 1984a, p. 122).

One of carnival's laws—and for Bakhtin perhaps the most important— is the seeming obliteration of the official, established social order, and "all the forms of terror, reverence, piety, and etiquette" connected to it (p. 123). In the second life of carnival, behavior, gesture, and discourse are freed. With the suspension of social hierarchies and conventions, a joyful "disorderly conduct" flourishes:

> Members of all social strata mix, joke and cavort in a mood of carefree abandon and "universal good humour." . . . Young men and women, each dressed in the clothes of the opposite sex, interact in a scandalous and provocative manner. Mock officials parade through the crowd, accusing people of horrible crimes and threatening them with arrest and punishment, which only elicits howls of laughter from the populace. (Gardiner, 1992, p. 44)

Carnival is life turned inside out and upside down. This disruption of life's routine, and especially the temporary abolition of powerful social hierarchies, allows participants to experience relations with each other and the world that are unavailable to them in everyday life.

A second important feature of carnival, then, is *free and familiar contact among people.* Physical and social distances between people are suspended in the jostling crowds. Constrained, coercive relations give way to ones based in freedom and equality. For Bakhtin, carnival is a context in which people take up and work out, even if only temporarily, new relations with others. Participants experience "in a concretely sensuous, half-real and half-play-acted form, *a new mode of interrelationship between individuals,* counterposed to the all-powerful socio-hierarchical relationships of noncarnival life" (Bakhtin, 1984a, p. 123).

But it is not only social relations that are transformed in carnival, not only people who get mixed and combined in disorderly ways. For Bakhtin, a "free and familiar" attitude spreads over everything, as values, ideas, events, and things are wrestled from their ordinary places in thought and practice, rearranged, and perceived anew. Carnival participants take up new relations not only with the people around them, but also with their world. A third feature of carnival, then, is a *playful, familiar relation to the world.*

This playful stance is signaled in numerous carnival practices, such as clothes being worn inside out, or underwear as outerwear; countless gestures, such as walking backward, standing on your head, showing your backside; the use of spoons and pots and other household objects as weapons of war in mock battles; and the creation of useless objects, such as buckets and barrels without bottoms. Bakhtin (1984b) warns against passing too quickly over these seemingly frivolous activities, and sees great import and possibilities in carnival's playful manipulation of the everyday world:

> It is a gay and free play with objects and concepts, but it is a play that pursues a distant, prophetic goal: to dispel the atmosphere of gloomy and false seriousness enveloping the world and all its phenomenon, to lend a different look, to render it more material, closer to man and his body, more understandable, and lighter in the bodily sense. (p. 380)

As the weight of the established social order and official ideology is lifted in carnival, unofficial and antiofficial discourse and activity emerge. The fourth feature of Bakhtin's carnival is this strong antiofficial current in the carnival sea—what Bakhtin calls carnival abuse, or *profanation*—which is expressed in the loud blasphemies, obscenities, and parodies that sound in the carnival square. Bakhtin emphasizes that carnival abuse is not personal invective aimed at other individuals. Instead, profanation has as its target the system of practices and ideas that oppress the people. Carnival abuse is directed, by the folk, at traditional authority and its "old truth," which are represented by "a Mardi Gras dummy, a comic monster that the laughing crowd rends to pieces in the marketplace" (p. 213).

The purpose or project of carnival abuse, however, is not purely negative. For Bakhtin, profanation is profoundly ambivalent—that is, both negative and positive, both destructive and regenerating. Carnival abuse kills the old so that the new can be born. This ambivalence is clearly seen in one of the most important rituals of carnival—the mock crowning and decrowning of the carnival king. In this ritual, a carnival king is crowned, only to fall prey later to carnival abuse in the decrowning, as he is stripped of his regal vestments, crown, and other symbols of authority, and subjected to ridicule and beatings:

> The ritual of the decrowning completes, as it were, the coronation and is inseparable from it (I repeat: this is a dualistic ritual). And through it, a new crowning already glimmers. Carnival celebrates the shift itself, the process of replaceability. . . . Under this ritual act of decrowning a king lies the very core of the carnival sense of the world—the pathos of shifts and changes, of death and renewal. Carnival is the festival of all-annihilating and all-renewing time. (Bakhtin, 1984a, pp. 124, 125)

This, for Bakhtin, was the lesson taught in carnival: things change. In carnival, the people laughed at ideas and practices supposed to be universal and eternal, and saw them for what they were—partial and contingent. And for the folk, for everyday people worn down by oppressive conditions, this was a hopeful lesson.

Active participation; free and familiar contact among people; a playful, familiar relation to the world—these carnival features are also important aspects of writing workshops. Profanation, however, is not: carnival abuse is muted in the writings of workshop advocates and is redirected, in sometimes disturbing ways, by children in their talk and texts. In what follows, I examine and evaluate these similarities and differences between workshops and carnival.

WORKSHOP AS CARNIVAL

Affirmations

The active participation of both students and teachers is a prominent theme in workshop literature.[2] In the opening sentence of one of the classics of workshop advocacy, Donald Graves (1983) asserts: "Children want to write. They want to write the first day they attend school" (p. 3). The problem, according to workshop advocates, is that traditional school practices do not encourage and sustain this active engagement with writing. In fact, traditional practices actually deny participation, demand passivity, and produce student resistance. Thus, workshop approaches emphasize the need for teachers to provide students with the opportunity to explore and learn about writing by writing. The primary strategy of these approaches is to grant students increased control (or *ownership*) over their own literate activities. According to Graves, writing workshop teachers

> Want the child to control, take charge of the information in his writing. Their craft is to help the child to maintain control for himself. That is the craft of teaching. They stand as far back as they can observing the child's way of working, seeking the best way to help the child realize his intentions. (p. 6)

For workshop advocates, students' increased control over their work helps them regain their interest in and commitment to expressing themselves in print.

In the workshop I set up with my third graders, this active participation—as well as the second feature of Bakhtin's carnival, free and familiar contact among people—can be seen in the primary activities of different parts of our daily routine.

Our workshop had a three-part routine. The first part—the *opening meeting*—lasted approximately five to ten minutes and was modeled after what Lucy Calkins (1986) calls minilessons. I used this time to teach, usually in a whole-class situation, the procedures and norms of the workshop and aspects of the craft of writing. This part of the routine placed students in a fairly traditional, passive student role. Interestingly enough, once students got used to the relative control they exercised in other parts of the workshop routine, they actively resisted the opening meeting. They persistently complained about it, claiming that it wasted *their* writing time; they called the opening meeting, among other derogatory things, the "opening infinity." Students even circulated a petition in the workshop that called for the opening meeting to be shortened. By March of that school year, we were calling the opening meeting the "opening minute," and I was consciously working to keep it short (Fieldnotes, 3–12–90).

The second part of the routine, lasting approximately 30 minutes, was *writing time*. This was the part of the workshop where children exercised the greatest control over their own work and movement. Children used this autonomy to engage in topics and stories that they found meaningful and to engage their peers and me in ways and at times that suited their work and the problems they faced as they wrote. If children needed to talk with someone about ideas they had for revisions of their stories, for example, they had the freedom to do so. They could go to their peers, or to me, or to Grace,[3] the regular classroom teacher, who often worked with us in the workshop. Primary activities for children during this time included brainstorming, drawing, drafting, revising, and editing texts; holding conferences with peers and the teacher; publishing selected texts; and reading. Children made choices during this time as to what they wanted to work on, with whom, for how long. My primary activity was to help students identify important stories,[4] revise their texts, and get their drafts ready for typing and publishing.

The final ten minutes or so of the workshop routine was *sharing time* (modeled after Graves and Hansen's [1983] "author's chair"). Sharing time was one of two primary ways for children's texts to go public within the classroom, to reach a larger audience than those in teacher and peer conferences. (The second was our workshop "library"—a few shelves at the back of the room where we housed children's published pieces. Children donated the books they wrote to the library for certain amounts of time so that other children could check them out and read them during writing time and other parts of the school day.) During sharing time, one or more children read their stories in front of the class, after which classmates and adults in the room shared their responses. Sometimes children shared finished pieces, which they had typed, illustrated, and bound between cardboard covers. Other times, children used sharing time to get help with planning or revising earlier drafts of texts.

Unlike traditional classrooms, our writing workshop did not lock children into passive spectator roles. Like participants in carnival, children experienced a blurring of performer and spectator roles in the workshop—"active" producing authors were not separated from "passive" consuming readers. Instead, children moved in and out of the roles of writer and audience. In both sharing time and the workshop library, child writers and their stories occupied spaces typically reserved for adults and official texts: in sharing time, the storytelling child replaced the teacher at the front of the room; in the workshop library, the child's book replaced the adult-authored and -selected text. And in contrast to traditional seating arrangements that bind children to desks and constrain peer relations—relations that flourish only at the edges, or in the absence, of the teacher's gaze (Erickson & Shultz, 1992)—writing time permitted movement and provided children with access to each other. At any given moment during writing time, children were clustered around desks, huddled under the bookshelves, or on the move to a conference with friends. Children could draw close to one another and engage each other in less constrained ways.

Writing workshop approaches encourage free and familiar contact among children. They also seek to lessen physical and social distances between teachers and students. As was suggested above in my discussion of our workshop routine, the teacher in the writing workshop is often *among children*, rather than in the front of the room.[5] In addition, workshop approaches encourage transformed teacher-student relations in their conception of teacher response to children's texts. A major concern of workshop advocates is helping teachers avoid falling into a typical classroom discourse that affirms the traditional social hierarchy between teacher and student, and silences students (Cazden, 1986).

Workshop approaches emphasize that teacher response should not simply evaluate student writing for grading purposes, but should seek to help students realize their own intentions in text. The teacher, once the sole initiator and audience/evaluator of student writing, now follows the child (Graves, 1983, p. 103), watching carefully for ways to encourage, support, model, and coach, at appropriate times, through response. Calkins (1986) would have teachers draw close[6] to students and become a genuine audience for them, an audience that is interested in what young writers have to say.[7]

> Our first job in a conference, then, is to be a person, not just a teacher. It is to enjoy, to care, and to respond. We cry, laugh, nod, and sigh. . . . Sometimes that is enough. Sometimes the purpose of a conference is simply to respond. Other times, if the moment seems right, we try, in a conference, to extend what the youngster can do as a writer. (p. 119)

In addition to transformed social relations, writing workshops support the active engagement of children with writing through the transformation of school writing tasks. And in this transformation of task, writing workshops, like carnival, encourage participants to take up a playful, familiar relation to the world. In at least three ways, workshop approaches support this playful stance by young writers.

First, workshop approaches reject traditional school writing tasks: they reject the grammar and usage textbook with its gloomy exercises, as well as tightly controlled teacher assignments. Second, writing workshops grant students wide powers to determine the topics, audiences, purposes, and forms of their texts, and support students in their choices. Rather than confront an alien, imposed world, children are asked to explore their own familiar worlds, and to do so in their own language; workshop advocates want "the schoolyard talk of children to become the poetry and prose of the classroom publishing house" (Willinsky, 1990, p. 200). As Nancie Atwell (1987) notes, workshop approaches have strong student-centered commitments in that "individuals' rigorous pursuit of their own ideas is the course content" (p. 41). But this "rigorous pursuit" is not necessarily "gloomy" or "serious": What are brainstorming, friendly conferences, and Peter Elbow's (1973) "free writing," but strategies for replacing an all too serious school approach to ideas and work with a playful, familiar one?[8]

Finally, writing workshops support children's playful, familiar stance to the world by bringing *writing itself* close to students and demystifying it. Rather than experiencing the typical, alienating school task of producing texts for evaluation purposes, children experience what it means to engage in the craft of writing, continuously and close up. They explore their experiences and world through drafting and revision, through seeing the effect of what they have to say on multiple audiences in the workshop. In the writing workshop, the process of writing and the role of writer are not kept at a distance, not denied children. And through writing, children begin to give shape and order to their world:

> By articulating experience, we reclaim it for ourselves. Writing allows us to turn the chaos into something beautiful, to frame selected moments in our lives, to uncover and to celebrate the organizing patterns of our existence. (Calkins, 1986, p. 3)

In support of children's active engagement with writing in the classroom, writing workshops encourage a free and familiar relation to the world by child writers, as well as free and familiar relations among workshop participants. Thus, it seems reasonable to compare writing workshops to carnival—a reasonableness that is only strengthened if you have ever actually experienced the noise, laughter, and incessant movement of active children in a writing workshop. Having made this comparison, however, I must immediately admit that if workshop is carnival, it is a rather pale, subdued one: one without the critical, sharp edge of Bakhtin's carnival. A carnival without bite.

An Orderly, Individualistic Carnival

Bakhtin emphasizes that a central aspect of carnival is its struggle against the official social order, its attempt to meet and disable established social relations and ideas with laughter, frank speech, and, especially, carnival abuse or profanation. Bakhtin's carnival has a strong antiofficial commitment that is simply absent from the writing workshops promoted by Graves, Calkins, and Atwell. These workshop advocates *do* provide important critiques of traditional school practices, but they seldom link these critiques and their proposals for classrooms to broader societal problems and struggles for change (Berlin, 1988). Workshop advocates make the teacher responsible for sharing a technical, craft curriculum with students that is aimed at supporting and enhancing children's writing processes. The content of children's writing is left up to individual children. Thus, any carnival abuse that does occur—and it does (I share some examples below)—is incidental, and represents an individual student's decision to challenge, parody, or criticize aspects of her world. But there is no systematic commitment within workshop approaches to the development and support of such critical practices by students.[9]

The bite of carnival is blunted in writing workshops, in part by the guiding visions workshop advocates have put forward.[10] In contrast to Bakhtin's images of a subversive, popular carnival, workshops have been guided by visions that are neither playful and critical enough nor collective enough to sustain profanation. As John Willinsky (1990) has noted, workshops are often portrayed in ways that recommend them as effective preparation for an official, corporate, workaday world, rather than as carnivalesque breeding grounds of playful, critical dissent and liberatory alternatives:

> [Workshops] would, after all, encourage independent and collaborative projects while drawing on peer support networks and conferencing with professionals to enhance the production values of the final and literate product. It can all sound and seem very marble and glass, office-tower work. While the editorial meetings at the classroom publishing house may not be a training ground for the leveraged buy-out artists, neither is it so removed from hustling projects and prospectuses for tomorrow's Wall Street jungle. (p. 19)

Bakhtin's carnival took place in the medieval market square, a site that shared something of the hustle and excitement, I suppose, of Wall Street. But Bakhtin's carnival was animated by a desire for freedom and equality, and celebrated a shared, communal abundance, rather than individual selfishness and greed.

For Bakhtin, profanation was a collective, critical response to an oppressive official world. A second aspect of workshop visions that undermines profanation, then, is their almost exclusive focus on and concern with the individual writer. Workshop approaches, as Mark Dressman (1993) puts it, "lionize lone wolves." The goals of workshop approaches are conceived of in terms of supporting individual children's intentions for writing, and project a vision of empowerment that is at odds with visions, such as Bakhtin's, that conceive of positive social change as the product of individual *and collective* struggle.

Workshop advocates have embraced an individualistic, Romantic rhetoric that abstracts writers and their texts from social context. James Berlin (1988) argues that this rhetoric *does* provide a powerful "denunciation of economic, political, and social pressures to conform" (p. 486). The problem for Berlin is that while this rhetoric champions resistance to dehumanizing forces and conditions, it is always (and only) individual resistance:

> The only hope in a society working to destroy the uniqueness of the individual is for each of us to assert our individuality against the tyranny of the authoritarian corporation, state, and society. Strategies for doing so must of course be left to the individual, each lighting one small candle in order to create a brighter world. (p. 487)

It is not that individual children do not try to light a candle every now and then in the writing workshop, for they do. There is carnivalesque student writing in the workshop that targets aspects of the official world and submits them to a playful disrespect and abuse. A fairly direct example comes from one of my students, Rajesh, who made his gym teacher into the main character of a story he wrote. This gym teacher was almost uniformly disliked by children in our workshop—according to them, he was quite mean. In his first draft, Rajesh used the teacher's actual name in the story; later, Rajesh changed the character's name to "Jud Coat." Rajesh's story:

> Far far away in the milky way galaxy there was a planet called MEAN. The things that lived on it were called Tickyes.
>
> One of the Tickyes came to our planet earth. Now, Tickyes can change shape. So it changed into a man called Jud Coat. He got a job at Clifford School. Jud was very mean! When anybody said Hi to him he would beat them up! And the worst thing was he kept multiplying. So somebody was going to have to get rid of him.
>
> And so I, Rajesh, stabbed him in the brain. ["the heart" in another version]

In his story, Rajesh targets an authority figure for criticism—"Jud was very mean!"—and abuse—"stabbed him in the brain" (a rather severe form of "uncrowning"?). Within the logic of the story, Rajesh's abuse clears the way, presumably, for a better world, one without the mean and multiplying Tickye, Jud Coat. Thus, in addition to the criticism and abuse of a powerful figure in Rajesh's official school world, the story has something of the ambivalent quality (both destructive and regenerating) that Bakhtin claimed characterized carnival abuse.

Other examples from our workshop were less direct, and seemed intent on testing implicit teacher and school definitions of acceptable topics for student writing. James, for example, told me on one of the first days of school that he was going to write about vomit (Fieldnotes, 8–30–89). Later, he and Ken wrote a story in which the two main characters—Kurt and Lisa (both named for children in this third grade classroom)—went to bed together. (Grace made James and Ken remove this event from their story before they shared it with the class.[11])

I point to these as examples of carnivalesque writing because they employ—even if without the conscious intention of the authors—one of the main strategies of carnival abuse that Bakhtin (1984b) examines in *Rabelais and His World*. Within the system of carnival images, both the earth and the lower body (the belly, bowels, and reproductive organs) functioned as grave for the old and womb for the new. In carnival abuse, then, a common tactic was to bring the high "down to earth" or *into contact or association with the lower body*, where the old would be killed, and then transformed and reborn. For example, one of Rabelais's characters in *Gargantua* and *Pantagruel* says that the shadow cast by a monastery's belfry impregnates women. This bit of carnival abuse works by associating the high, church tower, with the low, human body (male penis and pregnant women). Bakhtin argues that this abuse is not directed solely (or even primarily) at somewhat less than abstinent monks. Instead, "the monastic belfry, uncrowned and renewed in the form of a giant phallus . . . uncrowns the entire monastery, the very ground on which it stands, its false ascetic ideal, its abstract and sterile eternity" (1984b, p. 312).

James and his friends made the carnivalesque move of taking up as topics, within their official school writing, functions of the human body usually censored out of elementary schools or at least tightly controlled within them (as in sex education). They were young Rabelaises, with the similarity in strategy explained by the continuity of what they and Rabelais were up against—a Western tradition that separates mind from body, and that asks its students to "look higher" to the things of the mind. As James explained in his interview, he liked to "make serious things funny when the day's kind of going slow, and it's really not going, nobody's really having any fun" (Interview, 5–24–90). If you want to have a little fun, then one thing you can do is "look lower."

We can even hear echoes of carnival in an official workshop story told by Calkins (1991). When consulting with a school district on workshop approaches, one of her colleagues was met at the airport by a group of teachers who said that they were relieved that she had come, for they had embraced the writing workshop dictum that children could choose their own topics, and it had led to a problem. The problem? All over the school, students were writing about farts. Calkins's colleague told the teachers to tell the students to stop it, and the teachers responded with surprise—they could do that in a writing workshop approach? Calkins concludes:

> We laugh and think, "How silly." But it's not silly. It's sad. The problem is not that kids are writing about farts but that some of us have lost confidence in our ability to think for ourselves within the writing conference. (p. 228)

This is a fair enough moral to the story, especially given the larger context of low teacher status in our country and continued attacks on teachers and schools for putting the very survival of our nation at risk. But there is another moral, another problem lurking in Calkins's story. For me, the problem is that workshop approaches have an impoverished view of the ends toward which children might put their writing.

Workshop approaches have traditionally emphasized personal narrative. Children's writing remains cozily wrapped in a Romantic rhetoric that portrays it as "the innocent perceptions of children making individual sense of the world and their role in it" (Gilbert, 1989a, p. 199). Rajesh, James, and the children writing about farts were pushing writing in another direction that sought to upset and challenge aspects of their world—a direction that might, with support, grow into mature forms of parody or criticism.

I am sure that the students who were writing about farts were just "having fun." But surely part of the fun was knowing that, within the relative freedom of the writing workshop, they had found a topic to write about that made authority figures nervous. Writing workshops created a small space for expressing a part of life that is traditionally closed off in school, and the kids exploited that space. Calkins's colleague suggested that these children should just stop it. Maybe so. But the responses of Calkins and her colleague suggest to me that workshop advocates assume that once traditional social relations and school tasks are transformed in the writing workshop, students will have nothing left to challenge, criticize, abuse. These advocates tend not to consider the broader social, cultural, and political aspects of children's present and future lives, and pay scant attention to the benefits for children that might come with helping them oppose and criticize aspects of their world (Davies, 1993; Lensmire, 1994).

For Bakhtin, carnival abuse represented an explicit, collective struggle with an oppressive social order. At best, writing workshops, as currently imagined, might allow individual dissent. At worst, they might shut down even this, because their guiding visions provide no real resource for making sense of and responding to student resistance and opposition.

I have argued that writing workshop life contrasts to the "second life" of Bakhtin's carnival in its lack of profanation, even as individual students sometimes push their writing toward such an "abusive" end. I conclude my examination of workshops by articulating a problem that is common to both the writing of workshop advocates and Bakhtin's writing on carnival. Carnival abuse, it turns out, is not the only sort of abuse that is possible within the relative openness of carnivals and writing workshops.

A Shared Uncritical Populism

When the restraining hand of traditional authority was lifted during the actual carnivals of the Middle Ages and Renaissance, it was not only powerful groups and the official ideology that were in for abuse and mockery. Peter Burke (1978), for example, tells of a London festival in 1512 that became the occasion for the massacre and expulsion of foreigners. In certain instances, powerful groups used the openness of carnival to their own advantage; in others, relatively powerless groups *turned against even more powerless groups.*[12] Thus, even as carnival provides opportunities for freedom and equality and a protected space for antiofficial activity and discourse, it also "often violently abuses and demonizes weaker, not stronger, social groups—women, ethnic and religious minorities, those who 'don't belong'" (Stallybrass & White, 1986, p. 19).

I have been similarly concerned with how children treat one another in the carnival atmosphere of the writing workshop. Workshop advocates have assumed that the classroom communities students and teachers create for themselves in writing workshops will be supportive, productive ones *for everyone.* Lisa Delpit (1995) and Annette Henry (1996), among others, have questioned this assumption, especially for children who do not bring white, bourgeois meanings and values to the classroom. Thus, an important criticism that Peter Stallybrass and Allon White (1986) attach to Bakhtin's work on carnival—namely, that it embraces an uncritical populism—also holds for the writing of workshop advocates. Although these advocates are concerned that teachers take action to help students interact with each other in supportive ways—and their books contain helpful suggestions toward this end—ultimately workshop advocates overestimate (as I did) the effectiveness of such teacherly interventions. They overestimate the goodwill and openness that students have toward one another, especially across lines of social class, gender, and race.

My characterization above of free and familiar contact among children in the writing workshop was quite similar to the portrayals of peer relations in workshop literature. Atwell (1987), for example, who writes from her experiences as a teacher of eighth graders, asserts that "small groups [of students] form and disband in the minutes it takes for a writer to call on one or more other writers, move to a conference corner, share a piece or discuss a problem, and go back to work with a new perspective on the writing" (p. 41). My worry is that this openness and fluidity is only apparent, that beneath it are more stable patterns of peer relations among children that divide them, subordinate some to others, and routinely deny certain children the help and support that others receive from peers.

In our third grade workshop, when given the choice, girls worked with girls, and boys with boys. And the working-class children who lived in a large trailer park in the middle of this mainly middle-class community found themselves at the bottom of informal peer hierarchies of status and power in the classroom.[13] The experiences of Jessie—one of the children at the bottom of the peer pecking order—help us understand what is at stake here, and suggest the importance of appraising the peer relations that children work out with increased control over their own work and lives in workshops.

Jessie was the classroom's "female pariah," ostracized by nearly everyone "by virtue of gender, but also through some added stigma such as being overweight or poor" (Thorne, 1986, p. 175). Jessie was not small, and she came from the trailer park. Nearly everyone in the class, in their interviews, said that she was the least popular person in the class and the least desirable to work with. Bruce, for example, called her "idiotic, dumb"; John said that she stank; and Mary that Jessie never brushed her teeth. Only a few children said that they had worked with her in the class.

Grace and I often intervened in verbal fights between Jessie and other children. For example, when I arrived at school one Wednesday morning in February, I saw Robert and Suzanne, among others, yelling at Jessie, calling her "zit face."[14] I told them to stop it and made a point to walk up to Jessie and say good morning. Jessie paused long enough to say hello before continuing her own verbal defense and attack.

These verbal fights continued over the next few days. I wrote in my notes that "Jessie has been doing battle with Mary, Suzanne, Carol, and even sometimes, it seems, her friends Karen and Janis. But primarily with Suzanne and Mary" (Fieldnotes, 2–9–90). That Friday, I discovered that attacks on Jessie had found their way into print. When the children left for lunch, I noticed a child's text in the wastebasket. It was a story entitled, "The Killers in Mr. Lensmire's Class":

When we got into the classroom on Monday morning we heard
singing. It was Jil, Jessie, and Paul. They were singing a dumb song
that went like this: Let's get together, ya, ya, ya. Mrs. Parker
[Grace] was out of the classroom. Then Lisa shot Jessie in the back.
AAAAAH! Jessie said with a scream!

I do not know who the author was, or why he or she threw it away.
The attack on Jessie, however, was not the only one accomplished with the
piece of paper I found in the wastebasket. Below the story was a message,
written in cursive. The message read: "Mary you'r stupid!" It was written
twice, once in pen, once in pencil. On the back of the paper was: "To: Mary."
Perhaps Mary had written "The Killers in Mr. Lensmire's Class," had given
it to Jessie (or Jil or Paul) and had received a critical response to her work—
"Mary you'r stupid!"—which she threw away. In any event, Jessie was
being attacked in real life and as a fictional character.

   In her interview, Jessie said that she had only two friends in the class,
Janis and Karen (both from the trailer park). She said she sometimes had
conferences and shared her finished pieces with them, but usually she kept
her work to herself. Although she published four books during the year,
she did not share her books either during sharing time or in the workshop
library. She often had conferences with me, Grace, and the teacher aide. In
contrast to many of her classmates, she looked almost exclusively to adults
as audiences. When asked if there were things about the workshop
that she did not like, she said, "Some times I didn't like it was when
Mr. Lensmire couldn't get to me [for a writing conference]. I didn't like
that" (Interview, 5–30–90).

   There were other children who seemed to prefer adults as audiences
over peers, but most children in the workshop enjoyed and valued conferences with classmates, and shared their work with the class in sharing ses-
sions. In fact, because they valued their interactions with peers, the opportunity to conference and share their work with classmates was one of the
most positive aspects of the workshop for these third graders.

   But not just any peers. Children in the workshop *sought and avoided*
specific peer audiences in their daily interactions in the classroom. Children accomplished this by selecting whom they held conferences and
collaborated with on their stories.

   In general, *children worked with friends within gender boundaries*. All
children identified other children with whom they did and did not want
to have conferences—in other words, they made inclusions and exclusions,
and these differentiations were often associated with social class and gender differences. Karen, for example, spoke for children in the class when
she stated that "the boys like the boys, but the girls like the girls" for peer

conferences (Interview, 5–21–90). In Mary and Lori's interview, Mary was quite explicit (as were most children) about with whom she did and did not want to work: "I like working with Carol, Lisa, Marie, Sharon, Emily, Julie, and Suzanne. And I don't like working with the boys" (Interview, 5–31–90). Mary's list of girls, except for possibly Emily and Julie, is a fairly complete naming of the most popular girls in the class. She was also forthcoming about girls with whom she did not want to work and why. Mary said that "some of them had lice, they stunk," and she did not like their "styles" or their personalities.

> *Mary:* Most of them, and some of them are from the trailer park
>   and I don't like working with people who are from the trailer
>   park. . . . Like at first I thought that Lori was from the trailer
>   park before I went over to her house the first time.
> *Lori:* Thanks a lot.
> *Mary:* Well I did.

These valuations and devaluations of peers were acted out not only in patterns of association in the workshop, but also in stories that children wrote. Ken's story "All about Ken, Troy, and James," for example, embodied a hierarchy of characters that reflected social relations among boys in the class. Ken, Troy, and James were popular and powerful middle-class students in the workshop. In Ken's story, they were powerful dinosaurs who, in the first scene, dominate three other, smaller dinosaurs. The smaller dinosaurs were named for three other boys in the class:

> Me and Troy and James were running after three Pterodactyl. Their
> names are Robert and William and Bruce, and Robert and William
> and Bruce flew down. And then James ran up to get William and
> Troy ran up to get Robert. And Ken went up to get Bruce. And
> James said, "Look who I caught, a little squirt."

The story pitted three friends with superior size and strength as dinosaurs against three other classmates. These classmates were not Ken's friends, nor were they popular children. Two of the three were from the trailer park. One of them, William, was called a "little squirt" (he was one of the smallest boys in the class). Whatever Ken's intent, his story rehearses the sort of divisions and hierarchies that children created and experienced in the writing workshop.

Witness the list of characters Mary and Suzanne drew up for a play they had written. In the column to the left are the characters' names in the play. To the right are the names of children Mary and Suzanne thought should play those parts. Except for Joshua, who was Suzanne's fifth grade neighbor, all the children listed were students in this classroom:

Mouse	Maya
Princess	Marie
Stranger	Ken
King	Paul
Prince	Troy
Witch	Lori
Queen	Carol
Tower 1	John
Tower 2	Leon
Tower 3	Robert
Dancers	Suzanne and Joshua
Narrator	Bruce

Not all roles are created equal. Three characters (and only these characters) had no lines, had nothing to say in this play: Tower 1, Tower 2, and Tower 3. These roles were assigned by Mary and Suzanne to John, Leon, and Robert. Leon and Robert lived in the trailer park. John did not. Like Jessie, however, John was harassed a lot (unlike Jessie, he often cried and, on occasion, tried to bite those teasing him). As objects 1, 2, and 3, John, Leon, and Robert were to stand on stage from the beginning of the play to the end. Present throughout, but mute.

Jessie was from the trailer park, and she decided that it was too risky to share her stories with peers. After identifying children with whom she did not want to have conferences, Jessie described how she would feel if she were forced to do so:

> *Interviewer:* What would they do with your writing? How would you feel if you had to conference with them?
> *Jessie:* I would feel like a jar of slime. Being sat on.
> *Interviewer:* So maybe they don't treat you very well?
> *Jessie:* Yes. No, like getting cut in half. (Interview, 5–30–90)

Later, she said that she never shared in front of the whole class because they would make her feel the same way in that situation. Jessie declined my numerous offers to have her share with small groups of classmates.

From the beginning, I worked with Grace to make this writing workshop, and its conferences and sharing times, a safe place for children to write and share their work. We did many activities to help children respond to each other's writing in helpful ways. We talked often about how we needed to support and respect one another. Obviously, these teacher efforts were not enough to make the classroom a safe place for Jessie to share her work with peers. When asked why other people felt comfortable sharing their stories in front of class, Jessie said, "Because they have lots of friends."

One of the consequences of Jessie's relations with her peers was that her writing was never shared publicly in the workshop. Most children never encountered Jessie's retelling of "Sleeping Beauty":

> Once upon a time there was a beautiful princess, and her name was Jessie. One day, she was sleeping, and she heard a noise so she got up and went upstairs to the room upstairs. When she opened the door she saw a spinning wheel.
>
> When she was spinning at the spinning wheel, she poked her finger. Suddenly she fell asleep, and everyone fell asleep too. Just then a prince came.
>
> He snuck into the castle and found the princess and kissed her. And suddenly everybody awoke and the prince became an empire.

Jerome Bruner (1990) believes that the stories we tell and write "mediate between the canonical world of culture and the more idiosyncratic world of beliefs, desires, and hopes" (p. 52). Our stories represent a sort of compromise between, on one hand, how the world and we are supposed to be (given to us in the "canonical world of culture") and, on the other, what we might imagine our selves and world to be. When we tell stories, we retell old ones; we also manipulate and twist (and maybe sometimes even break and rewind) these stories in ways that express our "idiosyncratic worlds."

The twists Jessie gave to a more canonical version of "Sleeping Beauty" (from the Grimms [1883], for example), are heartening, and suggest a valuing of self, movement and activity, and power. Her crowned princess is named Jessie, instead of Rosamond. Jessie the author (as well as Jessie the princess) avoids altogether the angry witch who casts a death spell on the young princess, as well as the good witch who transmutes that spell to sleep. Jessie seems impatient with sleep—the princess "suddenly" falls asleep, only to be awakened almost immediately by a prince who "just then" arrived. In the Grimm version, the two live happily ever after together. Jessie's princess and prince may do likewise, but Jessie leaves this open. She is not content, however, with some sort of romantic bliss for the two. Jessie's version ends with the rise to power of her prince: He becomes "an empire."

Jessie's story may also be read against another "canonical world of culture"—the peer culture in which Jessie participated. The distance between the canonical peer world and Jessie's more "idiosyncratic" one is great. Jessie was not beautiful in the stories peers told about her. In that world, Jessie labored, moved, to avoid those who would cast spells that "cut her in half" and turn her into a "jar of slime." The school year was long, and she had little chance of friendly association (nor did she say she wanted it) with the powerful.

Jessie wrote herself and a vision of the world on the page, but others seldom heard her voice or saw her vision, at least not in the public spaces the workshop provided. Jessie thought that those spaces were for people with "lots of friends."

Most children had enough friends to make free and familiar contact with peers at least a mixed blessing. But there is an underside to children's relations that workshop advocates have not confronted. As in carnival, workshop participants sometimes use the free and playful space not to work out humane new relations, not to lampoon and discredit an unjust, official order, but to reassert and reinforce ugly aspects of exactly that same unjust, larger society. Abuse in carnival (and the writing workshop) is not, as Bakhtin wanted it to be, solely aimed at worthy objects of uncrowning. Some targets are chosen because they are easy targets, because already uncrowned, never crowned.

CONCLUSION

I have portrayed writing workshops as a form of carnival in order to highlight important, liberatory aspects of workshop life, and to identify problems that threaten to undermine its positive force. I have pointed to active participation; free and familiar contact among people; and a playful, familiar relation to the world as positive features of writing workshops that we should affirm. And I have questioned the individualistic and uncritical visions that guide current workshop approaches—visions that provide precious few resources for understanding, supporting, and criticizing the diverse ends to which children might put their talk and texts.

Workshop advocates have consistently criticized the traditional, controlling, fault-finding writing teacher, and have promoted instead a supportive teacher who finds meaning and who shares the craft of writing with students. The role they have imagined for teachers, however, assumes that teachers will never have to take up a critical stance in relation to children's work and the larger society within which children live and learn. Consequently, workshop advocates have drastically underestimated the sort of intellectual, moral/political, and aesthetic influence and leadership actually required of writing teachers if they are to be responsible in their work with children. In the next chapter, I examine strengths and weaknesses in how workshop advocates have imagined teaching and the teacher's role.

My third grade students and I created a community within the writing workshop, and children's writing emerged from and contributed to that community. The community we created was important for the experiences and learning of the children and teachers there. If, as Harris (1989) asserts, we "write not as isolated individuals but as members of communities whose beliefs, concerns, and practices both instigate and constrain, at least in part, the sorts of things we can say" (p. 12), then we had better pay attention to the communities we create in classrooms.

With the help of Bakhtin's work on carnival, I have tried to pay attention. Writing workshop approaches have the potential to contribute to the creation of more humane and just forms of life in school and society—a potential grounded in workshop commitments to help students engage in meaningful activity and take up open, learning relations with each other and the world. The absence of Jessie and her "Sleeping Beauty" from the public spaces of our workshop, however, reminds us that transformed peer relations represent both promise and problem in our progressive pedagogies. In the open, engaging, laughing, playing workshop-carnival, students have something to say about who speaks and is heard. We ignore what they are saying at our children's and our own peril.

NOTES

1. A brief treatment of Bakhtin's writings on carnival is difficult, because, as Gardiner (1992) notes, it is not easy to "disentangle what Bakhtin takes to be some of the more salient features of carnival, insofar as it constitutes a complexly interconnected and 'organic' whole" (pp. 45, 46). My characterization is based on Bakhtin's (1984a) own summary of carnival in *Problems of Dostoevsky's Poetics* (pp. 122–126). I omit discussion of what Bakhtin calls a "special category of the carnival sense of the world"—eccentricity—which permits the "latent sides of human nature to reveal and express themselves" (p. 123). Eccentricity is closely connected to two other features of carnival that I do discuss—free and familiar contact among carnival participants and a playful stance to the world, both of which function to liberate individual behavior and talk. Other helpful depictions of carnival are provided by Gardiner (1992) and LaCapra (1983). Not so helpful is Morson and Emerson (1990)—they seem very nervous about mixing with the folk celebrated by Bakhtin.

2. I emphasize active student participation in this chapter. In chapter 2, I explore the active role imagined for teachers by workshop advocates. See also Calkins (1986), pp. 163–165.

3. I have used pseudonyms for all children and adults who appear in my text. I have also used pseudonyms *within* children's texts when those texts name other people from the school. I have also done some minor editing of children's texts (mainly of spelling) when presenting rough drafts.

4. Throughout this chapter and the rest of the book, I focus on stories and ignore other sorts of texts (such as lists, reports, poetry) that children might produce in workshops. Workshop advocates tend to emphasize the writing of stories, especially accounts of personal experience. My own reason for emphasizing stories is their importance for our sense of our selves, others, and the world in which we live (see chapter 4).

5. I regularly wrote in my fieldnotes about how different children's expressions of affection and trust touched me. As an example, I made the following comments about Rajesh when he came to talk with me about trouble he was having with some classmates:

> Rajesh told me he had something "very important" to talk about with me. He said the words with feeling, and his voice broke several times. It didn't seem easy for him to talk to me about what he wanted to tell me.
>
> I like Rajesh a lot. He was one of the first kids I really started liking in the class. He was the first one to play with my long hair and tell me I should put it in a ponytail. He used to come over by me and sit on my leg while I talked to someone else at the table. So seeing Rajesh hurting hurt me too. But there was also a strategic, serious aspect to his words and tone. It seemed he felt he needed to persuade me of what he was saying. (Fieldnotes, 2–23–90)

I am not arguing that writing workshops are the only places where such interactions can occur. Rather, I am arguing that the relative openness of the workshop creates more opportunities for such interaction during class itself than does traditional pedagogy. See Lensmire and Price (1998).

6. Graves (1983) even attempts to represent workshop commitments to "drawing close" to students graphically, in a diagram of alternative roles that can be played by the teacher in writing conferences. Graves affirms the role of "advocate," which teachers embrace when they sit "next to the child" and position themselves so as to be "as close to equal height as possible" (p. 98).

7. This does not mean that workshop teachers are necessarily successful. A number of studies have indicated that it is actually quite difficult for teachers and students to break out of more traditional school discourse patterns. See Florio-Ruane (1991) and Ulichney and Watson-Gageo (1989) for helpful discussions of this problem.

8. I emphasize playfulness here because of Bakhtin's (1984b) continued association of certain forms of seriousness with the official ideology—an ideology that worked, in part, through inspiring fear: "In the eyes of Rabelais seriousness was either the tone of that receding truth and doomed authority, or the tone of feeble men intimidated and filled with terror" (p. 285).

9. See chapter 4 for my attempt to imagine such critical practices in workshops.

10. In the following discussion, I concentrate on the writing of workshop advocates and how they have conceived of workshops. I do not confront institutional aspects of schools and classrooms that undermine transformed social relations and tasks. Schools are not necessarily conducive to the sort of "adventurous learning" (Cohen, 1988) we might expect in more carnivalesque workshops, largely because of the pervasive demand that students be controlled and "orderly" within them.

11. See my extended discussion of this story, and the two sequels it inspired, in chapter 3 of Lensmire (1994).

12. See Gardiner (1992, p. 182) for a brief overview of historical studies of carnival.

13. Lines did not appear to be drawn by race or ethnicity: The four African American children in our classroom, and one whose parents were from India, did not form a subgroup—each of them worked and played primarily with white children within gender boundaries. Because I was primarily concerned with the inclusions and exclusions children made, and because I simply did not know much about how to interpret and theorize these aspects of the classroom, my analyses in Lensmire (1994) did not explore in any depth the meaning of race and ethnicity in the lives of children in this workshop; that does not mean that they were unimportant—see, for example, pp. 63–65.

14. Oral abuse using "zits"—in the form of "zit face" and "zit man" and "zit fit"—worked its way into several children's writing (see Lensmire, 1993). Thus, children's social relations were expressed not only in their talk and actions within and without the workshop, but also in their texts. An example is provided by Sharon and Carol, who described how certain boys used writing to tease girls in the class.

> *Sharon:* They use girls' names that, that liked other boys.
> *Intr:* Oh, and if—
> *Carol:* I think they used me with David, I'm not sure.
> *Sharon:* They used me with um, Ken.
> *Intr:* How do you feel about that?
> *Sharon:* I didn't like it.
> *Intr:* Why?
> *Sharon:* Because you don't like somebody to use your name.
> *Intr:* What, what can we do about that to change that?
> *Sharon:* I told them not to write it and I told them, and they, they kept on
>   writing and then I told Mrs. Parker and they erased my name out of
>   it. Then they would write the story, they kept on saying that, um, that
>   somebody in the story liked another person. (Interview, 5–30–90)

Boys wrote stories that named Sharon and Carol as characters. Within these stories, Sharon and Carol were supposed to like other boys in the class. In her study of gender relations among elementary school children, Thorne (1986) found that teasing such as "Carol likes David" was a "major form of teasing, which a child risks in choosing to sit by or walk with someone of the other sex" (p. 52) and that such teasing functioned to emphasize and maintain gender boundaries.

In the workshop, children created stories that teased other children by associating them, as story characters, with members of the other sex. They created stories that drew on gender arrangements (as well as social class differences) for their meaning and impact.

2

Teacher as Dostoevskian Novelist

In *Breakfast of Champions*, Kurt Vonnegut (1973) writes himself into his novel as a character. On a dark street among factories and warehouses, Vonnegut hails and introduces himself to one of his own creations, the character Kilgore Trout:

> "Mr. Trout," I said, "I am a novelist, and I created you for use in my books."
> "Pardon me?" he said.
> "I'm your Creator," I said. "You're in the middle of a book right now—close to the end of it, actually."
> "Um," he said. (p. 291)

Trout, of course, thinks that the man confronting him is crazy and asks if he has a gun. Vonnegut responds that he doesn't need a gun to control Trout, that all he has to do is write something down, and "that's it." When Trout still doubts his power, Vonnegut transports Trout to the Taj Mahal, then Venice, then Dar es Salaam, then the surface of the Sun, and then back to the dark city street with Vonnegut.

Trout collapses, and Vonnegut explains to his creation that although he has broken Trout's mind to pieces in the course of this and other novels, Vonnegut loves him, and wants Trout to experience a "wholeness and inner harmony" that Vonnegut has so far denied him. The Creator explains himself thus:

> I am approaching my fiftieth birthday, Mr. Trout. . . . I am cleansing and renewing myself for the very different sorts of years to come. Under similar spiritual conditions, Count Tolstoi freed his serfs. Thomas Jefferson freed his slaves. I am going to set at liberty all the literary characters who have served me so loyally during my writing career. . . . Arise, Mr. Trout, you are free, you are *free*. (pp. 293, 294)

Vonnegut makes himself disappear, and as he somersaults "lazily and pleasantly through the void" he hears Trout crying out to him: *"Make me young, make me young, make me young!"* (p. 295). But Vonnegut doesn't.

In this chapter I examine how teaching and the teacher's role in elementary and secondary school writing classes have been conceptualized by writing workshop advocates. To do this, I develop the metaphor of the writing teacher as Dostoevskian novelist. That is, I imagine the teacher as a novelist who creates a classroom/novel and takes up relations with student/characters; a *Dostoevskian* novelist, and not some other sort, because of the instructive similarities and differences between the project Dostoevsky pursued in his novels and the project workshop advocates want teachers to embrace in the writing classroom. At the heart of these projects—and a primary theme of this chapter—is the rejection of traditional relations between novelist and character, teacher and student, and the embrace of new ones.

Vonnegut's encounter with his character Kilgore Trout suggests just such a change in relations. Vonnegut wants Trout to be free from the purposes his Creator would bend him toward. No longer will Trout be tied to Vonnegut as serf or slave. Workshop advocates are similarly concerned that students be released from the tight control of the teacher, so that they and their writing might flourish. These advocates would have the teacher assert, with Vonnegut (1973), "I'm not going to put on any more puppet shows" (p. 5).

For Vonnegut, however, freeing Trout seems to mean *abandoning* him, severing the connection he had with Trout, rather than transforming the nature and quality of their relations.[1] This contrasts sharply with Dostoevsky's "method" of freeing his characters, which was based on approaching characters not as objects to be manipulated, but as subjects to be dialogued with. How students' freedom is imagined and achieved in writing workshops is a second important theme in this chapter. I worry about an element of abandonment in the freedom granted workshop students, even as workshop advocates call for humane, respectful, helpful teacher-student relations.

A third theme is teacher authority and power in the workshop. In their writings, workshop advocates have not done well with this theme, in part because teacher power is strongly associated with bad teaching, with the excessive control exerted over students by traditional teachers in traditional classrooms. In addition, student freedom is imagined exactly as freedom from teacher influence. At least two interrelated problems arise. First, workshop advocates often write as if teachers don't move with power in relation to students in workshops. Second, legitimate uses of teacher power are difficult for workshop advocates to imagine.

When Trout doubts Vonnegut's power over him, Vonnegut responds that all he needs to do is write something down, and that's it. And that *is* it, as Trout discovers. Trout's freedom, then, is just as much a product of Vonnegut's power and creative design as was his servitude. Similarly, I argue that students' relative control over their own writing in the workshop is a function of teacher design and power. That is, rather than being antithetical to student freedom, teacher power is necessary to assure it. At the same time, the student is always confronted with a teacher who could put his power to different ends. The teacher's control of students is certainly not as complete as the novelist's of her characters, but even the workshop teacher can just write something down—on a detention slip, a report card, a list of ability groups, a request for testing—and, within limits, that's it.

One final introductory note. In what follows, my characterization of Dostoevsky as a novelist is drawn from Mikhail Bakhtin's (1984a) portrayal of him in *Problems of Dostoevsky's Poetics*. I do not assume that my readers are familiar with Dostoevsky's writing. I do not criticize or evaluate Bakhtin's interpretation of Dostoevsky and his work—instead, I assume it. Having read Dostoevsky, I can say that, like many others, I find much of what Bakhtin has to say compelling and helpful in coming to a richer appreciation of the novelist's fiction. Here, however, I am interested in the fruitfulness of Bakhtin's portrayal of Dostoevsky and his project—not for making sense of Dostoevsky, but for making sense of teaching and the teacher's role in writing workshops.

A POLYPHONIC PROJECT

> In the ideal a single consciousness and a single mouth are absolutely sufficient for maximally full cognition; there is no need for a multitude of consciousnesses, and no basis for it. (Bakhtin, 1984a, p. 81)

Bakhtin named this ideal, this faith in the self-sufficiency of a single consciousness for "maximally full cognition," *monologism*. It was not Bakhtin's (or Dostoevsky's) ideal. Consolidated and promoted especially during the Enlightenment,[2] monologism "permeated into all spheres" of European culture and became a "profound structural characteristic of the creative ideological activity of modern times" (p. 82). Whether in philosophy or literature or the classroom, a monologic approach assumes that a single perspective is adequate for capturing, for telling the truth about, the world and the people within it. As Bakhtin put it, "Monologue pretends to be the *ultimate* word. It closes down the represented world and represented people" (p. 293).

Monologism closes down the world and people in at least three interrelated ways.

First, under monologic conditions, plurality is rendered superfluous, and difference, error. A plurality of meanings and values, a plurality of consciousnesses that perceive and know different things, is superfluous, because what is essential and true is apprehended by the single ideal consciousness. Whatever is not selected for inclusion is dispensable, unworthy of attention. And with the assumption that the ultimate word can be (or has been) spoken by a single mouth attached to the ideal single consciousness comes the implication that different words from different mouths must be wrong—difference is error. If you have the truth, you don't need or want anything else.

Second, monologism supports hierarchical relations between those assumed to know the truth and those who don't. For Bakhtin (1984a), monologism

> Knows only a single mode of cognitive interaction among consciousnesses; someone who knows and possesses the truth instructs someone who is ignorant and in error; that is, it is the interaction of teacher and pupil. (p. 81)

Bakhtin's criticism of the monologic novel emphasizes the subordination of characters and their voices to the novelist. Instead of diverse characters being the source of diverse points of view, they function to support and elaborate a single worldview, a single ideological position—that of the novelist. In his introduction to Bakhtin's *Problems of Dostoevsky's Poetics*, Wayne Booth (1984) notes that monologic novelists

> Never release their characters from a dominating monologue conducted by the author; in their works, characters seldom escape to become full *subjects*, telling their own tales. Instead they generally remain as objects *used* by the author to fulfill preordained demands. (p. xxii)

Substitute "teacher" for "author" and "students" for "characters," and we have the essence of workshop advocates' and radical educators' critiques of traditional classrooms. In traditional classrooms students are trapped within the dominating monologue of the teacher. They seldom escape this monologue to tell their own tales. Instead, their voices are subordinated to the preordained demands of teacher questions, assignments, tests. Paulo Freire (1970) calls this the "narration sickness" of traditional teaching.

A third way monologism closes down people and the world, then, is in this reduction of human beings to objects. This reduction, this reification, is accomplished both in the dismissal of what diverse peoples and individuals might know and speak and in the subordination of these people to those assumed to know the truth. Consider the story told by Donald Graves (1994) to suggest the origins of his approach to teaching writing. Graves reports that he experienced his "most traumatic failure" when, as a senior in college, he tried to use his honors thesis on Tolstoy's *War and Peace* to explore and make sense of experiences and problems then confronting him—the death of a close friend in Korea, being drafted, conscientious objection. If writing the thesis afforded Graves some insight and comfort, the reading his professor gave it did not.

> The professor wrote a cryptic response: "Please change your typewriter ribbon—D+." The only other marks on the paper highlighted thirty-six errors in grammar and punctuation (there were actually many more he didn't circle). He made no response to the content—my struggle with death, conscientious objection and the death of my friend. I felt humiliated and defeated. The Dean put me on academic probation. (p. 9)

Graves goes on to write that he "built a teaching career on that horrendous event" (p. 9).

For Graves, when his college teacher ignored the content of his paper, he ignored and dismissed Graves himself. The questions, the struggles, the particulars that made Graves who he was at that time were superfluous. It seems only his deviations from convention, his errors, were worthy of attention and response. In the process, he was dehumanized, reduced to an object of teacher evaluation and administrative sanction.

Dostoevsky rebelled against exactly this sort of dehumanization in his novels. For Bakhtin (1984a), the "struggle against a reification of man, of human relations, of all human values" was the "major emotional thrust of all of Dostoevsky's work, in its form as well as its content" (p. 62).[3] Against the reification of humans and human relations within monologism, Dostoevsky pursued what Bakhtin called *polyphony*:

> *A plurality of independent and unmerged voices and consciousnesses, a genuine polyphony of fully valid voices is in fact the chief characteristic of Dostoevsky's novels.* What unfolds in his works is not a multitude of characters and fates in a single objective world, illuminated by a single authorial consciousness; rather a *plurality of consciousnesses, with equal rights and each with its own world*, combine but are not merged in the unity of the event. (p. 6)

In contrast to the monologic novel, then, the polyphonic one features a plurality of voices and viewpoints. Furthermore, these voices interact with one another, and not in ways that subordinate some to others. The authority of the author's voice is decentered, distributed among voices with "equal rights and each with its own world." Each of these points—on the plurality of voices, their interaction, and the place of the novelist in the work—deserves additional comment.

When novelists talk about their work, they often report that their fictional characters seem to take on a life of their own within the process of producing a novel. There seems a certain wonder at this magic, as well as a gratefulness for the help (whatever the source) in making a certain character an interesting one. At the same time, the character's relative independence sometimes seems to become a source of exasperation, to become a problem: The writer has a story to tell, needs cooperative characters to tell it, and a particularly lively character is resisting.

Thus, when Vonnegut (1973) is on his way to meet his character Kilgore Trout, he is first confronted—unexpectedly, according to Vonnegut—by another of his creations: Kazak, a "volcanic" Doberman pinscher who, the novelist tells us, was a leading character in an earlier version of *Breakfast of Champions*. In that earlier version, Kazak was taught that "the Creator of the Universe wanted him to kill anything he could catch, and to *eat* it, too," which Kazak tried his best to do each night as he prowled the supply yard of the Maritimo Brothers Construction Company (p. 285).

Just before Vonnegut and Trout are about to meet, Kazak springs at Vonnegut from behind a pile of bronze pipe. Luckily for Vonnegut, Kazak's attack is blocked by a fence enclosing the supply yard, and, except for a rather extraordinary self-inflicted injury,[4] Vonnegut walks away from his encounter with Kazak unscathed. "I should have known," he writes, "that a character as ferocious as Kazak was not easily cut out of a novel" (p. 286).

In the end, Kazak was not cut out of the novel, and he rebelled against his Creator. For Bakhtin (1984a), one of the distinguishing aspects of Dostoevsky's work was that he created characters who were not "voiceless slaves," but *"free people*, capable of standing *alongside* their creator, capable of not agreeing with him and even of rebelling against him" (p. 6). Dostoevsky creates characters with *"fully valid voices"* that are not subsumed or captured under a "single authorial consciousness." Characters may, for monologic novelists, take on a life of their own under their creator's pen, but they will be used for elaborating the monologic novelist's worldview— they will ultimately be disciplined to the requirements of the novelist's story. For Dostoevsky, the character's task is exactly to articulate her own worldview, and this articulation—along with the articulation of other, diverse voices—is not in conflict with Dostoevsky's plan, with the story he would tell. It *is* the plan, the story:

> The entire artistic construction of a Dostoevskian novel is directed toward discovering and clarifying the hero's discourse, and performs provoking and directing functions in relation to that discourse. . . . the *"truth"* at which the hero must and indeed ultimately does arrive through clarifying the events

to himself, can essentially be for Dostoevsky only *the truth of the hero's consciousness*. (pp. 54, 55)

The "provoking and directing" functions of Dostoevsky's creative design are often achieved through placing the voices of characters in contact, in interaction, with each other. That is, a hero's truth emerges and sounds, not as the result of some inward exploration of ideas within an isolated, private psyche, but in dialogue with others' truths. For Bakhtin, Dostoevsky's ability to orchestrate and represent these encounters is grounded in how Dostoevsky, as a novelist, approached and related to his characters—not as objects to be talked about, but as subjects to be talked with.

I will be exploring this dialogic relation in more detail as I proceed, but for now I want to highlight one key aspect of it—a certain reciprocity of information, that Dostoevsky shared what he knew and said about the world and his characters *with his characters*. And because of this sharing, his characters were put in a position to respond to their creator, to agree and disagree with the truths Dostoevsky expressed about the world and the characters themselves.

In other words, Dostoevsky denied himself a privilege embraced by monologic novelists, what Bakhtin calls "authorial surplus" (p. 70). Put simply, "authorial surplus" points to novelists knowing more than their characters. For Bakhtin, monologic novelists hoard great stores of authorial surplus and use that surplus to pronounce monologic words about the world and characters they have created.

To show how this works, Bakhtin (1984a) analyzes a short story by the monologic Tolstoy, and imagines how it might have been rewritten by the polyphonic Dostoevsky (Tolstoy may have freed his serfs, as Vonnegut said, but for Bakhtin, Tolstoy never freed his characters). Bakhtin emphasizes how Tolstoy refuses the main characters of "The Three Deaths"—a noblewoman, a coachman, and a tree—access to the truths and meanings of the other characters' lives and deaths. The characters are connected externally, by being in the same place at the same time, but any internal connection, a "connection between consciousnesses," is denied them. Consequently, the lessons they might teach each other, as well as opportunities to embrace or reject these lessons, are kept from them.

> The noblewoman sees and understands only her own little world, her own life and her own death; she does not even suspect the possibility of the sort of life and death experienced by the coachman or the tree. Therefore she cannot herself understand and evaluate the lie of her own life and death; she does not have the dialogizing background for it. And the coachman is not able to understand and evaluate the wisdom and truth of his life and death. All this is revealed only in the author's field of vision, with its "surplus."

> The tree, of course, is by its very nature incapable of understanding the wisdom and beauty of its death—the author does that for it. (p. 70)

The final word on the lives and deaths of his characters, the ultimate word on who these characters were and what their lives meant, then, falls not with the characters, but with Tolstoy. Tolstoy's authorial surplus denies his characters the chance to make sense of, question, and challenge the judgments and evaluations made about them by the monologic author.

In the Dostoevskian rewriting of this story imagined by Bakhtin (1984a), the characters would be put into interaction with each other, and confront the others' truths and what these truths meant for their own. For Bakhtin, Dostoevsky wrote his novels in the form of a "great dialogue, but one where the author acts as organizer and participant in the dialogue without retaining for himself the final word" (p. 72). Dostoevsky does not reserve a privileged place for himself from which to *talk about* his characters. When Dostoevsky offers descriptions and evaluations of characters—through the voice of a narrator or another character—these judgments are made available to the characters, are brought to the characters' consciousnesses, and the characters have a chance to respond, to say yes, maybe, no, to what has been said about them. In contrast to the monologic novelist, Dostoevsky does not assume the privilege to say the final, objectivizing word about a given character—at a minimum, the character can say no to that word—and consequently, the character's future remains open, unfinished. And for Bakhtin, it is this open-endedness, this unfinalizability of human consciousness—its potential to learn, respond, rebel—that is its essence, an essence Dostoevsky respects and represents in his approach to characters in his novels.

That his characters speak with strong, "fully valid voices," that Dostoevsky does not take a privileged position in relation to these voices, does not mean that Dostoevsky has no position within the novel, or is inactive within it. Dostoevsky's characters' relative independence, their freedom from monologic words that determine them once and for all, is an aspect of Dostoevsky's creative design, just as the subordination of characters is an aspect of the monologic novelist's plan. The voices of Dostoevsky's characters can show themselves, be created, only with the intense, continuous dialogical activity of Dostoevsky.

> A character's discourse is created by the author, but created in such a way that it can develop to the full its inner logic and independence as *someone else's discourse*, the word of the *character himself*. As a result it does not fall out of the author's design, but only out of a monologic authorial field of vision. And the destruction of this field of vision is precisely a part of Dostoevsky's design. (Bakhtin, 1984a, p. 65)

The novelist moves with power in relation to the character in both mono-logic and polyphonic novels. The question, then, is not whether the novel-ist does or does not exert control, but to what end the novelist's power is put. In the monologic novel, the novelist's power is used to create a single worldview, praised and elaborated by the subordinate voices of subordi-nated characters. In the polyphonic novel, the novelist's power is used to create multiple, conflicting worlds embodied in the voices of diverse char-acters. The polyphonic novelist arranges situations and encounters with other characters that provoke and clarify the characters' own perspectives. In other words, the polyphonic novelist's power is largely expressed in-directly, in the orchestration of contexts within which the diverse voices of characters are called out, exposed, and developed. The novelist's power is used to develop, as much as possible, the "inner logic and independence" of *an other's* voice and perspective. Or, as Bakhtin put it: "The issue here is not an absence of, but a radical change in, the author's position" (p. 67). And that radical change is in the service of the destruction of a single, dominating, monologic worldview.

In contrast to an impoverished and deadening monologism, po-lyphony suggests great riches and liveliness, suggests the telling and shar-ing of truths suppressed in monologic settings. Workshop advocates have glimpsed this richness, this potential, as have we who are attracted to these approaches. Imagine the typical school cafeteria, with students in line to receive the homogenized food, while teachers watch over them, making sure that the students receive and eat this food in an orderly fash-ion. Then imagine a grand potluck banquet with students bringing their favorite dishes from home to share with others, as teachers direct the placement of pots and bowls on tables here and there. The students and teachers can be heard laughing, sometimes even shouting, "Try this" and "Oooh, that's too hot." Imagine a space, in school, alive with the sights, smells, tastes, feels, sounds of a plural world.[5]

Workshop approaches and Dostoevsky share a critique of dehumaniz-ing social relations under conditions of monologism. And in response, work-shop approaches take up a similar project in the classroom to the one taken up by Dostoevsky in his novels: the creation of a world in which multiple voices coexist and interact. In what follows, I explore how Dostoevsky and workshop approaches pursue the project of polyphony. I emphasize two aspects of Dostoevsky's and workshop approaches' method. The first is the radical *change in position* mentioned above—a change intended to promote dialogic relations between novelist and character, teacher and student. The second is the appropriation of the *adventure plot* as part of Dostoevsky's and workshop approaches' creative design.

FOLLOWING AND FREEING THE ADVENTUROUS CHILD

For Bakhtin (1984a), Dostoevsky effected a "small-scale Copernican revolution" (p. 49) with his decentering of the novelist's authority in his novels. That is, rather than be the center around which his characters must revolve, Dostoevsky positioned himself as a planet among planets, and interacted with them on the same plane. A similar decentering move is suggested by workshop advocates when they ask teachers to write with their students and to see themselves as members of a classroom community of writers where everyone teaches the craft of writing to everyone else. But the shift in the teacher's position is suggested most forcefully in a maxim from Graves (1983): *follow the child* (p. 103).[6] The workshop teacher will not dominate classroom discourse. Instead, the teacher will follow the child's lead, will watch and listen carefully for ways to support children's written expression:

> You want to teach. You want to help children create and take pride in their work, just as you have. You see teaching as another kind of authorship, which encourages students to express what they know. You observe them on the playground and overhear them talking. You sense the stories and ideas embedded in a single written line. You witness their expressive potential and help them realize their own intentions. You say to yourself, "This is why I want to teach." (Graves, 1994, p. 4)

Note that Graves calls teaching a "kind of authorship" that encourages students to "express what they know."[7] In contrast to traditional, monologic ways of proceeding in classrooms in which the content of students' lives is ignored and devalued, we see here workshop commitments to the familiar, the prosaic, as worthy of attention and writing. Furthermore, students would not be bound to the purposes for writing that a teacher might impose, but instead allowed to "realize their own intentions."

Workshop teachers, however, are supposed to do more than just allow students to express themselves. They are also to help students develop and clarify that expression. In grander language, Bakhtin (1984a) describes the parallel activity of Dostoevsky in relation to his characters, and links the success of this activity to the dialogic relationship Dostoevsky takes up with them:

> Dostoevsky's authorial activity is evident in his extension of every contending point of view to its maximal force and depth. . . . And this activity, *the intensifying of someone else's thought*, is possible only on the basis of a dialogic relationship to that other consciousness, that other point of view. (p. 69, emphasis added)

Workshop teachers seek to intensify each individual student's expression, and they do this by following the child, attending closely to the stories and ideas of children, and helping them make their expression and writing processes more effective. Indeed, the teacher's role extends beyond helping the student manipulate material already at hand. For Graves (1994), the teacher is also trying to see the *potential* "embedded in a single written line" (p. 4). In their interactions with students in classrooms, in observations of them on the playground and after school, workshop teachers get a sense of the possibilities for expression that individual children bring to the workshop. Again, we can affirm and enrich this workshop vision of the teacher's activity with Bakhtin's (1984a) words on Dostoevsky:

> He heard both the loud, recognized, reigning voices of the epoch . . . as well as voices still weak, ideas not yet fully emerged, latent ideas heard as yet by no one but himself, and ideas that were just beginning to ripen, embryos of future worldviews. "Reality in its entirety," Dostoevsky himself wrote, "is not to be exhausted by what is immediately at hand, for an overwhelming part of this reality is contained in the form of a still latent, unuttered future Word." (p. 90)

The "voices" Bakhtin evokes here are not primarily individual ones, much less the voices of individual children. Rather, they are the "social voices" of diverse groups of people expressing diverse ways of making sense of the world. But, for now at least, no matter.[8] The workshop teacher senses the unuttered future words of individual students, hears those ideas not fully emerged, supports the development of worldviews "just beginning to ripen." We might even note the resonances with John Dewey's (1899/ 1980) hopeful story, in *The School and Society*, of classrooms and schools as embryonic democratic communities. And this is why workshop teachers teach: not to enforce their own worldviews on children, but to help them develop and clarify their own ways of making sense of the world and their places within it.

The workshop teacher, however, is not only responsible for participating in dialogues with children. The teacher is also responsible for creating the context within which these dialogues, as well as dialogues among students, take place. In chapter 1, I conceived of this workshop context as a form of carnival. Here, I portray it as an adventure story (I ask that you suspend your disbelief for a short time as I make believe—despite the problems discussed in the last chapter—that all goes well with this story). In order to free student characters from the stifling restrictions of the traditional school plot, the teacher-as-novelist writes them into an adventure story. Within that adventure story, student characters pursue their interests and come to express themselves in a rough-and-tumble mix of people and ideas.

For Bakhtin (1984a), Dostoevsky rejected the traditional and respectable modes for plotting stories in his day because these plots trapped characters in tightly defined social roles or positions and in tightly determined sequences of events that would not allow them to engage in dialogue, would not allow for their humanness, their ideas, to be expressed and heard. Within such plots,

> The hero is assigned to a plot as someone fully embodied and strictly localized in life, as someone dressed in the concrete and impenetrable garb of his class or social station, his family position, his age, his life and biographical goals. His *humanness* is to such an extent made concrete and specific by his place in life that it is denied any decisive influence on plot relationships. It can be revealed only within the strict framework of those relationships. (p. 104)

Within such a strict framework, dialogue is largely impossible, and openness, possibility, are squelched by the tightly scripted lives of characters. We can draw analogies between characters in such plots and students in traditional classrooms and schools. Although workshop advocates do not take it up, we might, with the help of writers such as Bowles and Gintis (1976), Bourdieu and Passeron (1977), and Willis (1977), note schooling's contribution to the reproduction of social inequality in society, and call traditional schooling a plot in which a person's social position or category determines her relations with the institution and the people within it. In the traditional school plot, the humanness or uniqueness of the individual has no decisive influence on how the story turns out—schools serve society by sorting and classifying students according to what sort of "character" they are, as determined by "the concrete and impenetrable garb" of their race, class, gender, and age.

In the classroom, teacher and students within the traditional plot play dominant and subordinate roles, and students compete with each other for grades. Lesson plans script the motion and talk of participants, and within these lesson plans, the sequence of teacher question, student response, and teacher evaluation repeats over and over (Cazden, 1986). It is within these "strict frameworks" that teachers and students reveal themselves as human beings to each other—which means that they don't, much.

Dostoevsky and workshop advocates embrace an adventure plot, then, in order to free characters and students from tightly scripted lives.[9] The adventure plot is not driven by predetermined roles and conflicts. Instead,

> Problems dictated by [the hero's] eternal human nature—self-preservation, the thirst for victory and triumph, the thirst for dominance or for sensual love—determine the adventure plot. (Bakhtin, 1984a, p. 105)

The workshop student is involved in an adventure plot in at least two senses. As regards her writing, the student is encouraged to treat her own life as an adventure worth writing down. That is, workshop advocates emphasize writing grounded in students' own experiences and desires. Graves (1983) wants teachers to help students find "hot topics" with a "strong root of personal experience or affect" (p. 263). And Brenda Power (1995) notes that Calkins (1991), in *Living Between the Lines*, embraces an image of the child writer as a confessional poet who writes primarily about feelings and personal trauma. The problems and joys of being human are to be thematized by children, with children themselves determining the topics and stories to be taken up. Like the fictional hero within the adventure story, the workshop student's own intentions and experiences drive what happens within the workshop.

If the student's life outside the workshop is viewed as an adventure, his life within the workshop can also be so imagined. Not only are the child's intentions for writing freed within the workshop, but also his movements and associations. Dostoevsky's appropriation of the adventure plot helped him place his characters in "extraordinary positions" that exposed and called out their voices, their worldviews. The workshop functions similarly for the student: In contrast to the traditional classroom plot, the workshop-as-adventure-plot "connects him and makes him collide with other people under unusual and unexpected conditions" (Bakhtin, 1984a, p. 105). In other words, the student's social position, as student, does not exhaust who he is within the workshop, nor does it dictate his interactions with the world and others.

In the more fluid, contingent environment of the workshop, the student's interactions with the teacher and other students are not strictly and externally prescribed. The child can collaborate in writing a story with peers, get help from the teacher with a particular writing problem, seek out response to a draft or final copy of a story from classmates. For workshop advocates, the opportunity to take up alternative relations with the teacher and peers supports the child's development as a writer. The child's voice emerges out of the chance to write out of her own experiences and desires and to talk about them with others.

One final comment on plot in Dostoevsky's fiction and writing workshops. Bakhtin (1984a) notes that Dostoevsky's characters are not only *not* trapped in their social positions or biographies, they are also not trapped in a linear, tick-tock time:

> Dostoevsky makes almost no use of relatively uninterrupted historical or biographical time, that is, of strictly epic time; he "leaps over" it, he concentrates action at points of crisis, at turning points and catastrophes, when the

inner significance of a moment is equal to a "billion years," that is, when the moment loses its temporal restrictiveness. (p. 149)

Similarly, workshop teachers attempt to loosen the "temporal restrictiveness" of regular school time, where students' bodies and attention are directed not by engagement but by the bell (Lofty, 1992). That workshops provide students with *time to write* is a particular emphasis of Graves (1994). For Graves, writing can be considered an act of self-hypnosis: "I leave the external world in order to visit an interior world of memory, where I search the various caves of experience and recollection" (p. 120). In providing students time to write, then, workshops provide an escape from the press of a plodding, numbing school time. Workshops provide students with a precious resource—time to reflect upon, identify, articulate the inner significance of their personal experience.

Like Dostoevsky, workshop teachers use the loosening of linear time to concentrate action in the workshop on points of crisis, moments saturated with significance and meaning, turning points. How so? As noted above, workshop students are to focus their attention on "hot topics" and to write personal narratives grounded in strong feelings, personal trauma. The writing workshop concentrates action on points of crisis and turning points, then, in the sense that children are to explore and expose, in their writing, such moments in their lives.

Furthermore, workshops are set up to wait for, encourage, and support that moment, that *turning point*, when the student finally finds that "hot topic" worthy of exploration and exposition. I say "finally" because Graves (1983) admits that not every topic taken up by workshop students will be a hot one. He estimates that one topic out of four or five will be hot for any given student, and that in a class of twenty-four, "only five or six will be writing on 'hot' topics at any one time" (p. 28). As for the rest: "The rest put in their time, hoping for a breakthrough" (p. 257).

I have always appreciated the fact that Graves says this explicitly—it helps those of us who use workshop approaches feel less inadequate when things don't go so hot. But I would add that, for me, his and other workshop advocates' books suggest implicitly—in the examples of children's writing selected for inclusion, in their descriptions of workshop life, and in their prescriptions for teacher and student activity—that students' writing will actually be hot most of the time. Both imagined and enacted workshop worlds, then, like Dostoevsky's fiction, concentrate action on the charged experiences and breakthroughs of their adventurous heroes.[10]

In sum, the teacher-as-Dostoevskian novelist embraces an adventure plot to create a space, a context, within which student/characters are free to live and reflect upon and tell stories about an adventurous life. Within this space students escape the straitjackets of social position and institutional time, pursue their desires, mix with other adventurers, express their own unique worldviews. Within this space, the teacher abandons her monologue and follows the child, takes up new, supportive relations in order to encourage, amplify, intuit the beginning, whispered, unuttered future words of the next generation.

It's a good vision, a worthy one. And now we look closer. For even as this vision clarifies certain aspects of the workshop teacher's role and relationship with students, it blurs others. Below, I play with three meanings of "follow the child" to explore how this workshop maxim mystifies meaning-making, power, and responsibility in the workshop. And I pursue what the workshop attempt to free children from the constraints of social position and time might mean for their writing and learning. Beware: The adventure plot might be a trap.

FOLLOWING AND FETTERING THE ABANDONED CHILD

Let's begin with the meaning of "follow the child" suggested by "I don't follow you" or "Your meaning is hard to follow." In reading Graves's (1994) *A Fresh Look at Writing*, I was struck with how transparent he assumes children's writing to be. It seems that making sense of students' texts is always a relatively easy thing to do, if you have dedicated yourself to following the child. That is, if you are looking for spelling, punctuation, or grammar errors, you will not follow the meaning. But if you are looking for the meaning, you will find it.

Inasmuch as workshop advocates have incorporated research on children's writing development, made the teacher a student of the student and her writing, and organized writing conferences as places where students help the teacher understand what they are pursuing in their writing, this confidence is not wholly ungrounded. In my teacher education courses, for example, I have watched whole worlds of children's sense-making open up for future teachers as they read and discuss research on invented spelling. But workshop advocates have largely ignored at least two sources of difficulty in following the child's meaning.

First, a healthy body of literature documents the trouble teachers and students often have in following each other because of differences in culture, especially as these differences are expressed in language use.[11] A widely cited example is Sarah Michaels's (1981) account of how a young child named Deena was frustrated in her attempt to tell a story during sharing time. For Michaels, Deena and her teacher, Mrs. Jones, ran into difficulties because they brought different sharing styles to sharing time—

Deena a *topic-associating* style with links to African American culture, and Mrs. Jones a *topic-centered* style tied to European American culture. The result was that Mrs. Jones had difficulty following Deena, and therefore had trouble respecting and seeing the potential of what Deena was trying to do. And this in contrast to her success in following and supporting the expression of children who brought a topic-centered style to sharing time.

Second, workshop advocates have not confronted the fact that students, at times, will not want their teachers to follow their meaning. I remember a story a fellow educator told me about an elementary school in which the decision was made that teachers should use writing workshops to teach writing. Fairly quickly, however, administrators and teachers became concerned about the violence, and especially the killing, being represented in their students' writing. So a rule was made that there couldn't be any more killing in the stories students wrote. Soon, all over the school, fictional characters were getting "tapped" left and right. Tap, tap, tap. Imagine the writing conference in which the teacher, seeking clarity, asks what "tapped" means. Unless the child wants to rat, rat, rat on himself and his classmates, he'll have good reason to frustrate his teacher's desire to follow his meaning. For if the teacher follows his meaning, he's in trouble.

In this example, the first meaning of "follow the child" shades into a second, more troubling one, where "follow the child" suggests keeping her under surveillance, keeping an eye on her in order to control her.[12] One of the definitions of "follow" in my dictionary is "to pursue in an effort to overtake"—the "followed" student, then, may experience the close attention of the teacher, not as supportive and liberating, but as intrusive, coercive, maybe even threatening.

Consider Sarah McCarthey's (1994) story about Anita, an 11-year-old girl in a fifth/sixth grade writing class in New York. Anita's teacher, Ms. Meyer, was inspired by Calkins's (1991) discussion of writers' notebooks to have her students keep notebooks of their own. When it came time for Anita to write a piece from her notebook, she thought that she might write about her experiences at camp. Her teacher, however, worried that such a topic lacked impact and focus, that Anita would be unable to write about these experiences with the sort of powerful, personal voice workshop advocates call for. After an examination of Anita's notebook, Ms. Meyer thought that material concerning Anita's relationship with her father could be developed into a strong piece, and she encouraged Anita to write about that.

Ms. Meyer was in good workshop form. She carefully read Anita's notebook and tried to help Anita identify a topic—within the realm of Anita's own experiences—worthy of Anita's attention and effort. She didn't demand that Anita write about her father, but did *encourage* her to do so.

Now Anita had a problem, for she didn't want to write about her father. Anita hadn't spelled it out in her notebook, and Ms. Meyer didn't know: Anita didn't want to write about her father because he physically abused her and her brother. But how can she not write about this hot topic and still please her teacher, Ms. Meyer? And if she doesn't want to tell Ms. Meyer about her relationship with her father, she can't even reveal her real reasons for avoiding this topic.

Eventually, Anita came up with a fairly ingenious solution to her writing problem. She wrote about someone who was close to her, but not abusive—her grandfather. This allowed her to fulfill Ms. Meyer's seeming desire that she write about her relationship with an important person in her life, without exposing certain facets of her personal life to public scrutiny.[13]

Let me draw one moral from this story: Encouragement is sometimes not far from coercion in the classroom, given unequal power relations among teachers and students. The institutional authority of the teacher in school does not just go away when that teacher chooses to engage in alternative teaching practices such as writing workshop; it remains for the student to negotiate with the teacher, or work through, or (as in Anita's case) work around.

As I noted in the introduction to this chapter, workshop advocates don't attend much to teacher power and authority in the writing workshop—teacher power is something that bad teachers wield in traditional classrooms. In workshops, teachers assist children who—as Graves (1983) asserts with the first words of *Writing: Teachers and Children at Work*— "want to write" (p. 3). Children *want* to write, so there is really no need to remember that schooling is compulsory, and writing compulsory in the workshop. Workshop teachers *help* these children who *want* to write, so there is no need to worry about how teacher power haunts the "paradoxically intimate yet formalized relationship between teacher and student (always shadowed by its hierarchical and institutional context)" (Murphy, 1989, p. 175).

One of the strengths of imagining the workshop teacher as a novelist is that it makes teacher power harder to ignore. For we think of novelists as moving with power in relation to their characters, as creating and controlling them, as writing them into roles within a larger creative design that determines who they are, how they act, what they will be. The roles that workshops offer student characters *are* different from those offered in traditional classrooms. Workshop student characters enjoy an expanded control over the topics, purposes, audiences, and processes they will take up in their school writing. This expanded control, however, does not escape or transcend the teacher-as-novelist's plan, nor does it escape the larger context of schooling. Rather, the students' expanded control is part of the plan. In other words, students don't escape teacher power in the workshop; they confront a teacher power pursued with different means and toward a different end.

What end? My initial answer was the rejection of monologism, the embrace of polyphony. But it is time to reevaluate how well workshops, and especially the role they imagine for teachers within them, live up to the demands of a polyphonic project. I'll begin by pointing to a third meaning of "follow the child," where "follow" suggests accepting the authority of the child. More bluntly, that teachers should efface themselves, bow, before the child.

This may seem an odd direction, given the preceding discussion of teacher power in the workshop. However, as a maxim for teacher conduct, "follow the child" simultaneously enables and disables teacher power in relation to students. The disabling aspect comes in workshop advocates' fears that teachers will interfere in the meaning children are trying to make. That is, traditionally, teachers have not been reluctant to tell students what they should think and believe. Workshop advocates' response to this problem has been to restrict the conversations that are to take place around children's texts to questions of *technique, craft,* to how *effective* a given text is, given the intentions pursued by its author, given the meanings he is trying to make. The new and improved relations between workshop teacher and student are supposed to support, as Donald Murray (1985) put it, "professional discussion between writers about what works and what needs work" (p. 17). As for the intentions students are pursuing with their texts, as for the meanings and points of view and voices they are giving voice to, these are to be *left alone.* These are to be followed by the teacher, accepted, assumed in the technical work that follows of making student expression more effective.

Following the child, in this last sense of supporting and submitting to the intentions and meanings of student writers, creates problems for both teachers and students in workshops. For example, if certain students want to use their writing to make textual attacks on other students, should teachers really help these students make their attacks more effective? And what of racist, sexist, classist points of view expressed in student texts? I address such problems in later chapters. Here, I focus on two ways that the dialogic relations imagined by workshop advocates diverge from the dialogic relations taken up by Dostoevsky with his characters—divergences that undermine the workshop's polyphonic project.

First, as I noted earlier, a key aspect of Dostoevsky's relations with his characters was that Dostoevsky shared what he knew and thought about the world and his characters with the characters themselves. This sharing of what was normally the monologic novelist's surplus vision enabled Dostoevsky's characters to understand their own points of view and senses of themselves against the dialogizing background of other voices and truths. Workshop teachers, however, are not supposed to do this sort of sharing with their students. According to workshop advocates, teachers are to share what they know about writing as a craft, about how to go about writing and working a text so as to make its meaning clearer. As for the worlds and identities students create with their words, these are to be answered—not with questions, not with other world- and identity-evoking words—but with silence.[14]

Surely I am being too harsh here. After all, workshop advocates want teachers to share adult-authored literature with children, and want the workshop to overflow with the oral and written texts of children and teachers. The workshop is a place rich with the voices of children and adults.

Granted. But if you look at the interactions workshop advocates would have students take up with this abundance of texts, you see that they are all modeled on the third sense of "follow the child." That is, the meanings and values expressed in these texts are to be ignored, left unexamined and unquestioned. These texts are to be read not for what they might show us about the world and ourselves, but for what they might teach us about writing more effectively. In terms of my original discussion of polyphony, workshops feature a plurality of voices, but the intense interaction of these voices—the great dialogue—is greatly subdued. With help from Dewey (1922), we might imagine children's stories as dramatic rehearsals of ways of being and acting in the world, as first moves that would be answered with other stories, questions, criticisms, in a rich deliberation on what is and what could be, as well as on the powers, responsibilities, and pleasures of writing. Workshop advocates call for no such deliberation; indeed, their admonition to follow the child actually undermines it.

A second difference, then, between the dialogic relations within Dostoevsky's project and those within writing workshops is the conception of freedom these relations imply. The freedom of Dostoevsky's characters is based on their chance to respond to others' words about them and the world. That is, their freedom is achieved not through isolation but through engagement. Dostoevsky's characters are given access to other voices and points of view, and with that access, they can further develop their own ideas and resist being trapped by the words of others. In the end, the freedom of Dostoevsky's characters is grounded in their capability to say their own words about themselves:

A living human being cannot be turned into the voiceless object of some secondhand, finalizing cognitive process. *In a human being there is always some-*

thing that only he himself can reveal, in a free act of self-consciousness and discourse,
something that does not submit to an externalizing secondhand definition. (Bakhtin,
1984a, p. 58)

I do not doubt that workshop advocates hope to help children resist secondhand definitions and speak their own words about themselves. Given
the lack of deliberation built into the workshop about these words, however, it seems that children's freedom in the workshop is to be achieved
more by leaving them alone than by engaging them in dialogue with others.
In the name of not interfering in children's meaning-making, we may aban-
don them to it—free to express whatever they already are, but not helped
to escape it.

What, then, of our adventure story, given the trouble covered by "follow the child"? Does it have a happy ending?

Bakhtin (1984a) thought that Dostoevsky's "extraordinary artistic capacity for seeing everything in coexistence and interaction"—his ability to
represent characters who were alive in the moment of dialogue with others,
unpredictable, not determined by their pasts—was his greatest strength.
Bakhtin also thought (though he does little more than assert it) that this
greatest strength was also Dostoevsky's greatest weakness: "It made him
deaf and dumb to a great many essential things; many aspects of reality
could not enter his artistic field of vision" (p. 30).

What cannot enter, or at least has not entered, workshop advocates'
field of vision? Their adventure story attempts to help students escape
history. That is, the workshop context is intended to free students from the
bonds of social position and institutional time so they can be free to pursue their interests and interact with the world and others in unconventional
ways. However, inasmuch as this attempt at escape involves denials of
development, culture, and power, it may actually trap students in history,
rather than help them struggle with and against it.

I say denial of development despite the fact that workshop advocates
do tell stories of children's writing development. But these stories and the
morals workshop advocates draw for us are always concerned with the
development of skills, writing processes, with helping workshop teachers
help students craft more effective texts. Left unexamined are the meanings
and values students are developing within their texts, and how we, as
educators, might support the ongoing construction and reconstruction of
those meanings and values. To put the point differently: The workshop's
adventure story focuses attention on breakthroughs to hot topics. In the
absence of deliberation about those hot topics—in the absence of dialogue
and work that extends beyond consideration of technique—the development of students' ideas of self and the world is neglected.

I say denial of culture because workshop advocates have not recognized the ways that the voices and selves students bring to the workshop are bound up with the cultures they inhabit and that inhabit them. Thus far, workshop advocates have focused attention on the individual child and the individual child's "unique territories of information" (Graves, 1983, p. 22), as if children are not caught up in the meanings and values of family, community, and peers. Ironically, the exclusive focus on the individual—as separate, unique—child may actually undermine the workshop teacher's efforts to respect and follow that child. In order for Michaels's (1981) Mrs. Jones to respect Deena, she must "recognize" her, which, for Charles Taylor (1994), would involve knowledge of and respect for the cultures Deena draws on in creating her self and her voice. This is not to dispute the importance of teachers knowing and caring for students as individuals. But by not recognizing culture and its links to student identity, workshop advocates put at risk one of the adventure story's supposed benefits—rich, supportive interactions among teachers and students.

Finally, I say denial of power not only because of the denial of teacher power in the workshop as discussed above, but also because workshop advocates have not confronted what the ongoing struggles over meaning and value by powerful and less powerful groups in society might mean for the teaching and learning of writing in schools. Lisa Delpit (1995) reminds us that "ways of talking, ways of writing, ways of dressing, ways of interacting" are wrapped up not only with culture, but also with power, and that schools reflect the "culture of power." Furthermore,

> Success in institutions—schools, workplaces, and so on—is predicated upon acquisition of the culture of those who are in power. . . . The upper and middle classes send their children to school with all the accoutrements of the culture of power; children from other kinds of families operate within perfectly wonderful and viable cultures but not cultures that carry the codes or rules of power. (p. 25)

Rather than just follow children, Delpit would have teachers tell children about the "rules of power," the societally valued ways of communicating and presenting the self. Not because these valued ways are more worthy, but because they are the coin of the realm. Some children come to school with this coin in their pocket. Others will need to work in school to add it to the currency they bring with them from home—a currency declared devalued by powerful groups able to make such declarations. Delpit would have teachers risk embracing teacher power to tell children about the world so that they might be better prepared for it and defend themselves against it. She would have teachers be Dostoevskian novelists, and take up the challenge of sharing what they know, in order for their student/characters to be able to resist the secondhand definitions of others and speak their own word about themselves.

This is where the workshop adventure story begins to look like a trap, a setup, and the supportive, caring role imagined for the workshop teacher less supportive, less caring. We grant children a certain agency within the context of the workshop, by allowing children's interests, desires, experiences, to guide their own and teacher's work; but this agency might make it less likely that they gain access to resources they need to move with agency and power outside the workshop. Thus, the teacher's work within the workshop must be held responsible, not only to how it contributes to the ongoing activity of the workshop, but also to how it participates in the larger contexts of school and society. Or, to draw on the devastating example Kenneth Burke (1989) used to make the point that moral action must be read, interpreted, "identified" against the backdrop of larger and smaller contexts:

> The shepherd, *qua* shepherd, acts for the good of the sheep, to protect them from discomfiture and harm. But he may be "identified" with a project that is raising the sheep for market. (p. 186)

CONCLUSION

So where does this leave us? Certainly with more work to do imagining and revising the teacher's role and teaching in the workshop. Before suggesting a direction for this work, however, I want to point to a related problem requiring our attention—how we imagine and represent students and their learning and writing. As I wrote this chapter, I struggled with how closely to identify workshop students with Dostoevsky's heroes. In other words, if we imagine the teacher as a Dostoevskian novelist, do we then imagine students as Dostoevskian characters?

In the end, I did not emphasize this connection, because I am undecided as to how well Dostoevsky's characters listen to and learn from one another. Bakhtin's notion of polyphony features multiple voices in interaction with one another, but I remain unsure of the quality and consequences of that interaction. If Dostoevsky's characters don't listen well and don't learn much, then they are not great examples of our hopes for students. And if we take this negative view of Dostoevsky's characters, then polyphony does not seem so desirable—it becomes less a rich space in which to encounter new perspectives and try on alternative identities and more a babble of voices from characters who can't hear what others are saying.

I explore alternative, and more desirable, images of students and student voice in the next chapter. And then I return to the problem of teaching and the teacher's role in chapter 4.

John Willinsky (1986) argues that there is a problem at the center of the writing teacher's work. The problem is how to

> Bring together the opposing moments of art and education, providing *opportunity and motive for unfettered expression* and then the *imposition of reflection* upon it. (p. 13, emphasis added)

By writing students into an adventure story, and by constructing the teacher's role as one of supporting student/adventurers, workshop approaches have done quite well with the challenge of providing opportunity and motive for student expression in schools. Willinsky's "opposing moment" of reflection has been addressed only to the extent that children and teachers are to take up conversations about the effectiveness of student texts for *given* intentions, *given* meanings and values. The *examination, criticism, and reconstruction* of intention, meaning, and value—these have not been addressed in the books meant to support workshop teachers in their work with children.

We can expect that pursuing such work with students will make workshop teaching and learning harder. To examine and call into question important aspects of our identities and worldviews is a complicated and often distressing task. As we make workshops into sites of serious moral and political deliberation—as teacher and student questions and reflections focus attention (and sometimes criticism) on meanings and values held dear by workshop participants—the work of the writing workshop becomes more meaningful and more difficult, riskier.

The responsibility for promoting this sort of reflection cannot fall, ultimately, with students; this is what Willinsky signals, I think, with his "imposition of reflection." The imposition of reflection on student expression—a reflection adequate to what this expression means for their lives within and without the workshop—will be the action of workshop teachers taking up their power and responsibility on behalf of students and their voices.

For the opposing moments of art and education are not, ultimately, opposing. Rather, the unfettered expression of the student depends upon the imposition of reflection, on the teacher-as-Dostoevskian novelist who risks sharing everything with student/characters in dialogue. To not risk this dialogue, this engagement—to interpret "unfettered" as freedom from constraint rather than power to do—is to join Vonnegut in abandoning Trout to his old age. Only we will be abandoning children to their youth.

NOTES

1. Vonnegut (1973) writes, for example: "I think I am trying to clear my head of all the junk in there—the assholes, the flags, the underpants. . . . I'm *throwing out* characters from my other books, too" (p. 5; my emphasis).

2. Bakhtin (1984b) celebrates the Renaissance in *Rabelais and His World*; the Enlightenment is a time of loss—especially of the heightened sense of the relativeness of any single perspective or language. A similar story is told by Toulmin (1990) in *Cosmopolis*—philosophy is put on the path of relative sterility in the Enlightenment as it loses interest in the oral, particular, local, and timely.

3. The sentence continues: "under conditions of capitalism" (Bakhtin, 1984a, p. 62). Bakhtin thought that Dostoevsky had correctly recognized how the "reifying devaluation of man had permeated into all the pores of contemporary life, and even into the very foundations of human thinking"; he also thought that Dostoevsky did not understand the "deep economic roots of reification" (p. 62). A similar observation is made by Berlin (1988) about writing workshop advocates guided by what he calls an "expressionistic rhetoric." Berlin argues that these advocates are admirably concerned with individual agency and dissent, but that they do not understand how dissent and agency are actually threatened within a capitalist society.

4. Here, I follow the lead of my high school anthology of world literature.

While reading excerpts from Voltaire's *Candide* in this anthology as a high school junior, I got to the part where a young princess who has been unconscious awakes on the beach to find a moaning eunuch running his hands about her body. At exactly this point in this English translation of the narrative, the text shifted to Italian (I think) to represent the eunuch's words. I didn't usually read footnotes in high school, but I did this time and found in the footnotes that the eunuch was complaining about not having any testicles. Oh, my.

When Vonnegut (1973) catches sight of Kazak leaping toward him out of the corner of his eye, and before he has even had time to register the danger consciously, his body prepares for fight or flight. At this point in the novel, Vonnegut writes a page or so of technical description of the messages to glands, the hormones secreted, the bodily responses to this threat. He reports:

> Everything my body had done so far fell within normal operating procedures for a human machine. But my body took one defensive measure which I am told was without precedent in medical history. It may have happened because some wire short-circuited or some gasket blew. At any rate, I also retracted my testicles into my abdominal cavity, pulled them into my fuselage like the landing gear of an airplane. And now they tell me that only surgery will bring them down again. (p. 289)

This happens just when Vonnegut is on his way to free Trout, and I continue to wonder if Vonnegut is suggesting that, in freeing his characters, he is emasculated. Is he suggesting that the novelist who doesn't have control of his characters is less of a man/novelist? And if we decide he is suggesting this, what might this mean for our explorations of the teacher as novelist? Is a teacher who embraces less control over students less of a teacher?

I tried discussing this incident and these questions with colleagues at an informal presentation of my ongoing work on this chapter. Their responses—mostly stony silence, but also the giggling of a few of my friends—suggested that I adopt my high school anthology's strategy of putting such things in a footnote. Sorry that I don't write Italian.

5. One problem with this cafeteria feast metaphor, as I have deployed it here, is that it suggests that that which children bring with them from home and community—languages, ways with words (Heath, 1983), stories—are always already finished and not in need of work, development, and reconstruction. Rather than already prepared dishes brought to school to share, then, we might imagine children bringing what they had to school—Moll et al. (1992) would have educators help them bring it—and the feast being prepared there.

One irony of my use of feast imagery is that when superficial versions of multicultural education are enacted or criticized—what Henry (1998) calls "'chomp-and-stomp' celebrations" (p. 87)—food is usually involved. I invoke food and feasting here in Bakhtin's (1984b) sense of carnival abundance; and as opposed to the dry, thin diet of stories and cultures too often provided in the official curriculum of schools.

6. Workshop and whole language advocates have suggested the teacher's new position in the classroom in a number of ways; for example, teacher as exemplar, or coach, or cheerleader (see Willinsky, 1990, p. 204). I have chosen to focus on "follow the child" because, for me, this maxim best captures what we would want to affirm about workshop conceptions of teaching. However, with some work, it can also be used to help us understand some of the limitations and problems with workshop conceptions.

7. Graves (1994) does not develop the idea of teaching as authorship here (or elsewhere, to my knowledge). He does, however, talk about writing and teaching as *twin crafts* that "demand constant revision, constant reseeing of what is being revealed by the information in hand; in one instance the subject of the writing, in another the person learning to write" (Graves, 1983, p. 6).

8. Only for now, because this easy appropriation of "voices" as individual voices will eventually get us into trouble. Workshop advocates' nearly exclusive focus on the individual child—as separate and unique—ignores how students' voices and selves are bound up with the social voices of home, community, popular culture, and peers. I take this up later in the chapter, as well as in chapter 3.

9. Dostoevsky, in addition to adventure plots, used dream stories and aspects of Menippean satire and carnival to free characters—see Bakhtin (1984a).

10. Not that I was necessarily less guilty of this in my own book (Lensmire, 1994) on writing workshop approaches. I also concentrated action on charged experiences within the workshop, but I usually concentrated on negatively charged ones.

11. See Au (1993) for an admirable, concise characterization of this work and what it might mean for literacy education.

12. Drawing on Foucault (1977), theorists such as Walkerdine (1990) and Hogan (1990) argue that teacher power works differently in traditional classrooms and sites such as writing workshops—a difference captured in the contrast between "sovereign" and "disciplinary" power:

> Sovereign power is negative and judicial and functions through rituals of terror and repression; disciplinary power is positive and constitutive, a "technique" that operates through highly localized political "technologies of power" based on the accumulation of knowledge of individual subjects. (Hogan, 1990, p. 12)

Or, as Walkerdine (1990) puts it, "[N]ot overt disciplining but covert watching" (p. 22).

That is, teacher power in progressive pedagogies is grounded in exactly the sort of surveillance suggested by "follow the child"—the teacher watches, gathers information, quietly manipulates. As for the child:

> The child whose nature we are to monitor with our all-knowing, all-seeing gaze is to be calculatedly liberated, controlled into freedom. (Walkerdine, 1990, p. 118)

13. Graves admits that when we ask children to write of their personal experiences, we are, as teachers, asking them "to undress." His solution to this problem? Teachers are also to undress, by sharing their writing with children (see Gilbert, 1989b, p. 24). We are to ask children to undress, and say, don't worry, we'll undress, too? The metaphor Graves jumps to is apt, but his response suggests how little he has considered the vulnerability of students in the face of workshop teachers' institutional authority and power.

14. Although Walkerdine has not, to my knowledge, written directly about writing workshop approaches, I don't think that she would be surprised by this relatively quiet, subdued workshop teacher. Indeed, it is what you would predict from her work. For her, progressive education is founded on images of the active child developing in a nurturing, but essentially passive, environment. Furthermore,

> The teacher is part of the environment (part of the woodwork?). She is there— it is her watchful and surveillant presence which facilitates the mastery and independence, the self-reliance of the child. She must know thirty children "as individuals." She is passive; the child is an active body. . . . She is the price paid for autonomy, its hidden and dispensable cost. (Walkerdine, 1990, p. 119)

We can see workshop advocates struggling to write the teacher out of this passive role. Calkins (1986), for example, feels the need to argue explicitly that both the student *and the teacher* should be active in the writing workshop—which, when you think of it, is a little odd. Another example is when Graves (1994), in his preface to *A Fresh Look at Writing*, asserts that "although listening to children is still the heart" of workshop approaches, he and other workshop advocates now know that "right from the start, teachers need to teach more" (p. xvi).

3

Voice as Project

If I am good enough and quiet enough, perhaps after all they will let me go; but it's not easy to be quiet and good, it's like hanging on to the edge of a bridge when you've already fallen over; you don't seem to be moving, just dangling there, and yet it is taking all your strength.
—Margaret Atwood, *Alias Grace*

This chapter is an extended meditation on alternative conceptions of student voice. I begin with the version of voice put forward by workshop advocates—*voice as individual expression*. Workshop advocates emphasize students' desire to express their unique selves in writing, and how traditional writing instruction frustrates this desire. Then, I examine a second conception—*voice as participation*—that comes from advocates of critical pedagogy. These advocates, including Paulo Freire (1970, 1985), Henry Giroux (1988, 1991), and Roger Simon (1987), call for critical dialogues among teachers and students. Within these dialogues, student voices would sound and be heard.[1]

I have learned much about voice and student expression from writing workshop and critical pedagogy advocates. There are serious problems, however, with how they have imagined talk and writing in schools. I propose an alternative conception of student voice, an alternative that affirms the strengths of workshop and critical pedagogy conceptions, as well as responds to their weaknesses. My goal is to conceive of student voice in a way that more adequately recognizes the complexities and conflicts of student expression, so that we might, as educators, better support the flourishing of student voices in schools.

One final note: In her novel *Because It Is Bitter, and Because It Is My Heart*, Joyce Carol Oates (1990) tells a brief, provocative story about school writing that I will use as a starting point and connective thread for my reflections on student voice.[2] Among other things, the story reminds us that if all student voices have fared relatively badly in schools, *certain* student voices have fared worse than others. Let me restate my hope for my alternative conception of voice: that it do justice to the challenges confronting all students who would speak and write in schools, but especially those who find no easy place within the dominant meanings and values of our racist, sexist, and classist society.

VOICE AS INDIVIDUAL EXPRESSION

Oates's novel is set in a small town in upstate New York in the 1950s. A young black man, Jinx Fairchild, is one of the main characters. At one point, Jinx writes a 500-word composition for his senior English class, and then receives comments and a grade from his white teacher, Mrs. Dunphy. The assigned topic of the composition is "I Believe" and we learn that Jinx

> Spends days on the assignment . . . writing and rewriting in a ferocity of concentration nearly as singleminded as his concentration on basketball. The effort is exhausting. He has never thought of the words on paper as expressions of the soul, the voice on paper a silent rendering of his own voice.

Unlike Mrs. Dunphy, workshop advocates do not believe in assigned topics because this takes control over the writing away from students, does not allow them the privileges of "real authorship." For workshop advocates, authors are writers who have control over, have "ownership" of, their writing processes and texts. Real authorship involves "the fullest engagement of the writer in the production of meaningful text under the pressure of her conscious and unconscious intention" (Gilbert, 1989b, p. 15). Students-as-authors, then, have the right to identify, for themselves, topics and purposes for writing that are worthy of their time and effort.

Jinx would make workshop advocates proud. Although Mrs. Dunphy assigned the topic for Jinx's writing, he obviously deemed the "I Believe" theme worthy, and pursued it through multiple drafts and revisions across a number of days. More important, however, was his realization that "words on paper" could be "expressions of the soul." Jinx's struggle to have his voice on paper be "a silent rendering of his own voice" is exactly the struggle, the task, that workshop advocates would have students take up in writing class.

Workshop approaches emphasize the work of finding your own voice in your writing. Finding your voice involves looking to your own experiences for what it is you have and want to say. There are strong affinities here to Ralph Waldo Emerson, Henry David Thoreau, American Romanticism, a celebration of experience and an individualistic, nonconformist strain. The image is one of burrowing deep into subjectivity, past the "mud and slush of opinion, and prejudice, and tradition" (Thoreau, 1854/1960, p. 66) to discover your authentic nature, and a voice that expresses who you are.

Workshop advocates assume that students are best able to find their individual voices when they are allowed to pursue their own intentions and topics, rather than those forced on them by the teacher. From this perspective, the "I Believe" theme worked for Jinx because it put him on the terrain of personal experience and belief, allowed him to draw on personal resources he might otherwise not be able to draw upon. In this sense, for workshop advocates every bit of authentic writing, every act of real authorship in the writing classroom, pursues the "I Believe" theme. And if it weren't for traditional teaching methods, students would gladly be pursuing this theme and themselves in print, because they want to.

> Children want to write. They want to write the first day they attend school. This is no accident. Before they went to school they marked up walls, pavements, newspapers with crayons, pens or pencils . . . anything that makes a mark. The child's marks say, "I am."
>
> "No, you aren't," say most school approaches to the teaching of writing. (Graves, 1983, p. 3)

No you aren't, said Mrs. Dunphy to Jinx Fairchild:

> When he gets the composition back he sees to his shame that his teacher Mrs. Dunphy has marked it in red: numerous grammatical errors, several run-on sentences, a fatal "lack of clarity." The grade is D+, one of the lowest grades Jinx Fairchild has received in English, in years.
>
> "Ordinarily I would give a paper like this an F," Mrs. Dunphy says, peering up at Jinx over her half-moon glasses with a steely little smile of reproach. "You know the rule, Jinx, don't you? No run-on sentences."
>
> Jinx mumbles, "Yes, ma'am."
>
> "Didn't I write it out on the blackboard? NO RUN-ON SENTENCES."
>
> "Yes, ma'am."

With her talk of error and inadequacy, Mrs. Dunphy dismisses Jinx's attempt to express his very soul on the page as quickly and easily as she might erase from the chalkboard what seems her dominant goal for school writing: NO RUN-ON SENTENCES.[3] Of course, we are on very comfortable ground here, as we root for Jinx against Mrs. Dunphy, a teacher who would ignore the personal meaning he is trying to make and focus on mechanical correctness. And as long as we stay on this ground, as long as our story is essentially a Romantic one of bad social institutions threatening the development and integrity of the unique individual, workshop notions of voice remain relatively safe and persuasive.[4] Schools and teachers have denied and shut out individual student voices (remember Donald Graves's story about his college professor in the last chapter?); writing workshops will allow them to sound.

But Mrs. Dunphy herself disrupts this satisfying story as she continues her response. It seems that her teacherly expectations for an "I Believe" theme have brought out a little of the workshop advocate in her. She was looking for Jinx's soul on the page, and she didn't find it. The "fatal lack of clarity" that at first appeared to be just another disparaging comment aimed at Jinx's writing performance may actually be questioning the relation of Jinx to his paper. For Mrs. Dunphy, the relation is not one of clarity—this paper just doesn't seem a clear reflection or representation of Jinx's authentic nature:

> "And is the argument wholly your own?" Mrs. Dunphy asks doubtfully. "It doesn't sound . . . like something you'd be thinking."
>
> Jinx Fairchild stands silent as if confused. Is the white woman accusing him of cheating?
>
> As if reading his thoughts Mrs. Dunphy adds quickly, "The tone of the composition doesn't sound like *you*, Jinx. It sounds like somebody else, a stranger. It isn't *you*. And the thinking is muddled and incoherent." She gives a breathy little laugh, uneasy, annoyed: this tall hooded-eyed Negro boy standing there so unnaturally still.

We may interpret this exchange as the continued dismissal of Jinx's individuality—a dismissal accomplished this time not by pointing to the mechanics of his writing, but to the content of his essay. The teacher tells the student to tell her who he is and what he believes. He does. She tells him, from her position of authority and across lines of gender and race, "No, that's not who you are." The problem, then, is not that she asks him to express himself on the page, but that she does not accept or recognize Jinx when he does.

I will return to this problem later. At this point, I want to note one final aspect of voice for workshop advocates that Mrs. Dunphy's interactions with Jinx Fairchild help us understand.

Workshop advocates do not only assume that it is a good thing to tap into and express your real, authentic self in your writing, and that when you do, your writing is marked by your own unique voice. They also assume a particular conception of the *self* to be tapped: a traditional Enlighten-ment conception, in which the self is imagined to be stable, coherent, uni-tary, and autonomous. Thus far, workshop advocates have paid little attention to the serious criticisms this conception of self has received from, among others, psychoanalytic, feminist, and postmodernist theorists (see Flax, 1990), and they have ignored alternative conceptions which, while certainly differing in important ways, point to a vision of the self as dy-namic, in process, multiple, and formed within social relations with others. As John Willinsky (1990) has noted: "The self, as that pure and singular essence of our being, is no longer a reliable figure in the psychological or literary landscape" (p. 220).

This unreliable figure carries workshop advocates' conception of voice, and we can see this figure at work in Mrs. Dunphy's response to Jinx. Mrs. Dunphy assumes that Jinx's self is stable and unitary—certainly solid enough that she can say no, that's not Jinx, when she reads his paper. She denies that multiple voices might sound within Jinx's subjec-tivity, that what "sounds like somebody else, a stranger" might be part of Jinx's self.

Mrs. Dunphy may call him Jinx, but she really only knows the "Ice-man"—a persona that Jinx adopts, rather consciously, while in school and other times when he is challenged or threatened. Jinx is also known as Ice-man on the basketball court. The Iceman is cool, unflappable, aloof, always in control.[5] But Jinx's self is not exhausted with the Iceman—alongside this persona, there is Verlyn (not Jinx) Fairchild, whom his mom loves and talks with at home; and beneath and in interaction with Verlyn and the Iceman are other postures, other voices, that make up Jinx.

Mrs. Dunphy was looking for *Jinx*. When, instead, she got a glimpse of something else, something less unitary, less finished, she could only be confused, disturbed, name it "muddled and incoherent."

Mrs. Dunphy assigned an "I Believe" paper. She assumed that Jinx would sit down, take a look at himself and what he believed, and write that down. The image is consistent with workshop images of writers at work—the solitary writer and his struggle to have the voice on paper be a "silent rendering of his own voice." What Mrs. Dunphy and workshop advocates don't seem to recognize—or more precisely, what their concep-tions of voice, self, and writing make difficult to consider—is that writers are not really isolated individuals, but embedded (for Jinx, embroiled) in important social relations with others that influence the work of writing and creating a self.

For in Oates's novel, one of Jinx Fairchild's problems is that he is tied to two white youths in complex relations of love, solidarity, hate, and vio-lence. Where Mrs. Dunphy looks for a calm reflection on the "I Believe" theme, Jinx looks to figure out his place and moral responsibility within these relations, as well as in relation to society and God. Oates shares only a small part of Jinx's composition with her readers, and we can't tell if this part is from an early or late draft, from beginning, middle, or end of the piece. We *can* tell that Jinx is seeking to define himself and his place in the world:

> I believe we are born with Sin on our head and must labor to cleans ourselves all the days of our life. It is not a matter of Gods punishment but of Conscience, if there is no God nor Jesus Christ there is still Human Conscience.

Jinx labored to have the words on paper be "expressions of the soul," and this is the goal that writing workshop advocates promote for individual students in writing classrooms with the idea of personal voice. We should affirm at least two related aspects of this conception of voice.

First, the workshop emphasis on student voice entails a commitment to taking students' experiences and meanings seriously, in contrast to traditional pedagogies that often run roughshod over personal meaning in the name of teacher control and convention. I agree with Willinsky (1990) that to "diminish the potential for individual meaningfulness in students' work is a denial of their basic humanity" (p. 209). The goal of voice is part of workshop attempts to humanize writing pedagogy through the acceptance and encouragement of students' assertions of "I am" in the classroom.

Second, the idea of voice is linked to the vision of students bringing themselves—their interests, energies, hopes, experiences—to their work with texts. Again, in contrast to traditional pedagogies that not only put meaning at risk in the classroom, but often demand passivity from students, workshop approaches ask students to pursue, vigorously, the purposes and topics that the students themselves find compelling. For workshop advocates, there can be no personal voice in the writing without this personal investment, this active student engagement.

But even as we affirm workshop commitments to personal meaningfulness and engagement, we must recognize that the particular conception of voice workshop advocates have put forward—one grounded in an Enlightenment conception of the self and images of the solitary writer pursuing personal meaning—can get us into trouble. The workshop conception of voice assumes a stable, preexistent self that can be more or less expressed in writing. But as Joseph Harris (1987) notes: "Writing is not simply a tool we use to express a self we already have; it is a means by which we form a self to express" (p. 161). It is not just that one conception of voice is more or less accurate. The conception of voice we bring to our work matters for

how we think about Jinx and our students, for how we might judge
Mrs. Dunphy's and our own responses to student texts, for how we imagine our teacher practice and responsibilities.

VOICE AS PARTICIPATION

> A radical theory of voice represents neither a unitary subject position unrelated to wider social formations nor the unique expression of the creative
> and unfettered bourgeois subject. Both of these positions depoliticize and
> dehistoricize voice by removing it from the arena of power, difference, and
> struggle. A radical theory of voice signifies the social and political formations that provide students with the experiences, language, histories, and
> stories that construct the subject positions that they use to give meaning to
> their lives. (Giroux, 1991, p. 100)

For writing workshop advocates, voice is tied to the notion of a unitary, unfettered individual self. Advocates of critical pedagogy assume no
such self. For them, the self is a social entity, created out of the cultural
resources at hand. This does not mean that the self is envisioned as *determined* by these cultural resources, in the strong sense that the passive individual becomes whatever is dictated by an overpowering social context. The
resources available—the experiences, languages, histories, and stories—
obviously constrain the possible selves you can become. At the same time,
they provide possibilities, possibilities that can be more or less consciously
worked in the creation of a self. As Caryl Emerson (1986) expressed it: "One
makes a self through the words one has learned, fashions one's own voice
and inner speech by a selective appropriation of the voices of others" (p. 31).

The space for choosing, for fashioning yourself out of the words of
others, is enlarged by the complexity and plurality of the social contexts of
our lives. No environment, as John Dewey (1922) noted, is "all of one piece"
(p. 90). Instead, society is marked by a multiplicity of cultures, meanings,
and values—a state of affairs that is inscribed in language, and that Mikhail
Bakhtin (1981) named "heteroglossia":

> Thus at any given moment in its historical existence, language is heteroglot
> from top to bottom: it represents the co-existence of socio-ideological contradictions between the present and the past, between different epochs of the
> past, between different socio-ideological groups in the present, between tendencies, schools, circles and so forth, all given a bodily form. (p. 291)

For Bakhtin, these diverse languages of heteroglossia[6] express particular
stances or positions on the world; they represent "forms for conceptualiz-

ing the world in words, specific world views, each characterized by its own objects, meanings and values" (pp. 291, 292).

Critical pedagogues would have us pay attention not only to the plurality Bakhtin evokes with his notion of heteroglossia, but also asymmetries of power across this diversity (note Bakhtin's "top to bottom")—asymmetries that enable powerful groups to define their own particular "ways with words" (Heath, 1983) as *the* valued ways in society. As Giroux (1991) notes,

> What meanings are considered the most important, what experiences are deemed the most legitimate, and what forms of writing and reading matter, are largely determined by those groups who control the economic and cultural apparatuses of a given society. (p. 93)

Dominant groups determine dominant meanings, but not without a struggle, and never once and for all. In fact, the larger educational and political project of critical pedagogy is exactly to empower students to engage in this struggle over meaning—in solidarity with the wretched of the earth; in the name of social justice, equality, and democratic community; and in preparation for and as part of transformative social action.

We are ready to characterize voice in critical pedagogy. I develop this characterization through a series of contrasts between voice in critical pedagogy and voice in writing workshop approaches.

For workshop advocates, voice signals the unique expression of the unique individual. Voice serves to distinguish individual writers from other writers. For advocates of critical pedagogy, voice signals *participation*, an active part in the social production of meaning. Voice points to the "discursive means whereby teachers and students attempt to make themselves present and to define themselves as active authors of their own world" (Simon, 1987, p. 377). If the workshop sense of voice is evoked with the contrast, "my words versus someone else's words," then the contrast to voice within critical pedagogy is silence, where silence points to oppressive conditions that keep certain people from speaking and being heard. Rather than emphasize the attempt to distinguish yourself from others, voice, here, emphasizes inserting yourself and your texts into public spheres.

Another way to contrast writing workshop and critical pedagogy versions of voice, then, is in their relations to liberty and popular sovereignty. The workshop commitment to voice is concerned primarily—perhaps exclusively—with liberty, especially freedom of thought and expression. A commitment to liberty is certainly part of critical pedagogy, since students need to be free to express themselves in the classroom in order to participate in the moral and political project envisioned by its advocates. But in the main, voice in critical pedagogy is linked to the goal of popular sovereignty, to making power "accountable . . . to those affected by its exercise" (Bowles & Gintis, 1987, p. 4). Critical pedagogy wants students to be active participants in the construction of their worlds, rather than trapped in the meanings, subjectivities, and forms of authority determined by powerful others.

Voice also serves different functions within the pedagogical schemes of writing workshop approaches and critical pedagogy. For workshop advocates, voice is the goal, the desired endpoint, for any given piece of student writing. It is a criteria with which to judge the success of the writing and instruction—without that stamp of individuality, without the "imprint of ourselves on our writing" (Graves, 1983, p. 227), the text and teaching have failed. Within critical pedagogy, however, voice is less a goal or endpoint in itself, and more a necessary precondition for the collective work to be done. Voice is a starting point in critical pedagogy, in at least two ways.[7]

First, advocates of critical pedagogy assert that the affirmation of students' own experiences, languages, and stories is crucial. For these advocates, traditional pedagogies belittle and alienate students by not respecting and working with the ways that they make sense of themselves and their worlds. Giroux and McLaren (1986) write that "student experience is the stuff of culture, agency, and identity formation and must be given preeminence in an emancipatory curriculum" (p. 234). To not affirm and respect student voices is both morally wrong, because it disparages who students are and what they know, and strategically a mistake, because students will resist becoming active partners in teaching and learning. Thus, student voice is a starting point in the sense that this moral and political project cannot be a truly participatory project without it.

Second, voice is a starting point in that it provides resources, material, with which the classroom community can work. Student voices make available a multiplicity of texts that can be examined, learned from, and criticized. Critical pedagogy's emphasis on voice, then, is very much in the spirit of Dewey's (1899/1980) call for a transformed recitation. In the traditional recitation, individual students answered teacher questions for the purpose of displaying what they had memorized from the textbook in a competition for teacher rewards. Dewey imagined a different sort of recitation, one where the recitation

> Becomes the social clearing-house, where experiences and ideas are exchanged and subjected to criticism, where misconceptions are corrected, and new lines of thought and inquiry are set up. (1899/1980, p. 34)

Workshop advocates sometimes recognize the wealth of material made available by student voices, but their responses to this wealth diverge, again in instructive ways, from those of critical pedagogues. Witness Donald Murray (1985):

> I read their papers and share their surprise in their own diversity with them, and I know that I will never burn out, that I will never lose my excitement at my own and students' explorations of our world with the writing process. (p. 248)

I find two aspects of Murray's comments striking. First, how private this is, in ways reminiscent of Jinx's conversation with Mrs. Dunphy. There is no sense of student papers somehow contributing to a collective project—the projects here are private ones, pursued by individual students, supported by the teacher. In another piece, Murray (1979) writes of his work as "this strange, exposed kind of teaching, one on one" (p. 14). The exposure of this teaching is, of course, the exposure of authentic selves in the writing and response. The wealth of student voices is, here, a private wealth, accumulated by individual students and teachers in private transactions.

Second, there is no hint in Murray's comments that teachers will ever have to take up a critical position vis-à-vis the meanings of student papers. Above, he talks of surprise and excitement. At other times Murray (1985) points to pursuing, with students, "professional discussion between writers about what works and what needs work" (p. 140). Never is there mention of the need for teachers to question or criticize students' intentions and meanings.

Pam Gilbert's (1989a, 1989b, 1994) work helps us understand this lack of criticism. She argues that the notion of personal voice ties student-written text and student tightly together. One consequence of this merging of text and student is that student texts "are seen to be so closely aligned to the individual child and that child's original making of meaning that they are 'beyond criticism'" (1989a, p. 198). In other words, any criticism of the meanings students make with their texts can be interpreted as a disparagement of or attack on the person of the student.

Gilbert also points to some of the trouble that this notion of personal voice gets us into. For what if the authentic student voice is, say, a sexist one, as in an example Gilbert (1989a) provides from a Year 5 writing workshop in Australia? Gilbert tells of the collaborative effort of four nine-year-old boys who wrote themselves into their own fictional story of war and destruction. They made themselves heros, of course. They also wrote seven girls from the class into their tale. Six of these girls were given stereotypical roles in the story—"having 'affairs,' holding hands with boys, getting married, saying 'I love you'"—before becoming victims of war, disposed of in "reasonably ugly ways" (p. 200). The one girl to escape the textual fate of stereotype and death happened to be the biggest girl in the class. In the story, she jumps on top of the enemy and scares them off for a while. She also gets called "Super Blubber." As Gilbert notes:

> No need to kill off this female: her size and aggression have effectively excluded her anyway (what worse fate for a girl than to be called Super Blubber?). (p. 200)

Are we, with Murray, to marvel at this exploration of the world by these young boys, and help them make it work even more effectively?

Critical pedagogy's conception of voice leads us into no such trap. Individual students' voices are assumed to arise from a social self, shaped and created in social contexts of great diversity. Student voices are formed within an oppressive society that privileges the meanings, values, and stories of some over others. These voices—like the voices of teachers, curriculum developers, novelists, scientists—are assumed to be necessarily partial, to express a particular position on the world that will make possible certain understandings and constrain others. Consequently, critical pedagogues say over and over again that student voices must be not only affirmed, but also questioned:

> Developing a pedagogy that takes the notion of student voice seriously means developing a critically affirmative language that works both *with* and *on* the experiences that students bring to the classroom. This means taking seriously and confirming the language forms, modes of reasoning, dispositions, and histories that give students an active voice in defining the world; it also means working on the experiences of such students in order for them to examine both their strengths and weaknesses. (Giroux, 1991, p. 104)

Critical educators may certainly marvel at the diversity of experiences, languages, and stories that are called forth with the elicitation and affirmation of student voice in the classroom. But there is also work to be done—a critical testing of these voices for what they can teach us, and how they can and cannot contribute to the creation of a better world. For Murray and other workshop advocates, the sounding of the voices of heteroglossia in the classroom is already a better world. Maybe so. For advocates of critical pedagogy, this heteroglossia may, unfortunately, sound too much like the already existing world, and be in need of criticism and revision.

It should be obvious that I find much about critical pedagogues' treatment of voice attractive and persuasive. I value their assumption of a social self developing in multicultural contexts. I affirm, in general, the critical democratic project they are pursuing. Within this perspective, voice is conceived of in terms of participation in the construction and reconstruction of the world and the ways in which we make sense of it. Advocates of critical pedagogy avoid an uncritical stance in relation to student meaning-making, while at the same time asserting the worth and importance of student voice to an emancipatory educational project.

But writing workshop and critical pedagogy versions of voice also share important similarities (Giroux, 1987). Both would have student voice flourish in the classroom. Both seek to humanize teaching and learning in schools through the acceptance and affirmation of student voice. Both encourage the active exploration by students of their worlds, rather than passive submission in the face of teacher control and knowledge.

Unfortunately, critical pedagogy and writing workshop conceptions of voice also share at least one serious weakness: neither has come to grips with what *conflict* among voices—conflict generated among students, between teachers and students, and within individual students—means for the actual production of speech and writing within classrooms.

VOICE AND CLASSROOM CONFLICT

Workshop advocates' characterization of writing as a personal, individual activity does not quite jibe with their prescriptions for how workshops should be set up and run. On the one hand, the guiding image to which students and teachers should aspire is the solitary author in pursuit of personal meaning in private writing projects. On the other hand, workshop advocates would organize writing classes as very sociable places to write and learn—supportive writing conferences with peers and the teacher, collaborative writing projects, regular opportunities to receive response and affirmation from the class during sharing time, and classroom libraries housing student-written work make for workshop settings that are rich with possibilities for social interaction. Indeed, Courtney Cazden (1994) thinks that workshops may be considered "one of the best examples of 'cooperative learning,' so widely advocated for today's schools" (p. vii).

In other words, workshop rhetoric champions the solitary writer even as its actual classroom practices throw the student writer into multiple, shifting relations with peers and the teacher. Workshop advocates finesse this incongruity by emphasizing individual student choice and initiative—the student writer is portrayed as being *in control*, as the one who determines when and how to interact with others. Nancie Atwell (1987), for example, writes that "within the structure of a writing workshop, students decide who can give the kind of help they need as they need it" (p. 41). In this way, workshop advocates can assume both that real writing is intensely individual and that student writers need help from others.

Of course, these others are always eager to help, and give the help the writer wants and needs. Within advocates' stories about workshops, then, there is little room or cause for consideration of social conflict. And there's the rub. For actual workshops are not so conflict-free. Certainly, easy access to peers and teachers within workshops provides student writers with opportunities for social interactions that can support and inspire. But these social interactions are also openings for conflict and risk, opportunities for peer and teacher audiences to push back on student voice in negative ways. While there truly are important differences between workshops and Phil Jackson's (1968) traditional classroom, his "crowds, praise, and power" remains an apt description of workshop life.

At first glance, it seems silly to assert that advocates of critical pedagogy are, like workshop advocates, blind to conflict. For they are not. The cultural politics perspective these theorists bring to their work on voice assumes conflict across and within the border lines of social groups in society; assumes struggles over identity, meaning, and authority. Furthermore, critical pedagogues know that asymmetries of power give dominant groups the advantage in these struggles and that certain groups—women, people of color, the poor and working class, gays and lesbians—find themselves in continuing conflict with the dominant meanings and values of society.

Conflict penetrates deep into the discourse of critical pedagogy. Unfortunately, it does not penetrate to the level of face-to-face (or in your face) interactions in the classroom. Somehow, the sweaty, painful struggles over meaning that characterize life in society are left at the classroom door of critical pedagogues. Within, the sharing and questioning of student voices leads, it seems, to cool conflicts of interpretation, rather than heated confrontations between actual people who, in expressing themselves, find themselves at odds.[8] And while advocates of critical pedagogy recognize asymmetries of power across classroom participants (specifically, teacher and student), they have, as Elizabeth Ellsworth (1989) notes, "made no systematic examination of the barriers that this imbalance throws up to the kind of student expression and dialogue they prescribe" (p. 309).

In the end, neither workshop nor critical pedagogy advocates embed student voice in the immediate social context of the classroom, and consequently they ignore important problems and issues attending the speech and writing of students there. Writing workshop advocates embed voice in the inner context of the author's intentions, desires, dreams, experiences; when the social context of the workshop is considered at all, it is only as a

friendly one that supports individual students' expression. Critical pedagogues embed voice in politics and history writ large, rather than within the
local meanings, values, and relations—the micropolitics and microhistories—
of particular classrooms.

Peers loom large within classrooms that forego tight control of student
bodies and talk. As discussed in chapter 1, individual students do not perceive and experience these peers as an undifferentiated and uniformly
supportive whole. Instead, they confront multiple peer audiences that they
judge to be more or less supportive, more or less hostile, to their attempts
at expression. In other words, children, especially unpopular children, feel
there are serious risks involved in writing for and speaking in front of
peers—risks to their sense of self, to what they value and care about, to
their social standing in relations with others. Children's responses to these
risks include seeking out certain classmates as audiences and avoiding
others. Some choose not to insert themselves and their texts into public
spaces—spaces created exactly to allow all students' voices to sound and
be heard within the classroom community.

If conflict and risk attend peer relations in classrooms, they also attend relations between teacher and student. Students and teachers confront
each other in a social context and institution not necessarily conducive to
free and open talk and writing. Gilbert (1994) reminds us that "a number
of different and incompatible discourses mesh at the site of the classroom
because schools are about—among other things—selection and sorting,
discipline and punishment, knowledge and control" (p. 264). Workshop
advocates and critical pedagogues recognize this to the extent that their
stories and criticisms of traditional pedagogy are concerned, in varying
ways, with student voice taking a beating in its struggle with powerful
teacher and curriculum voices. That complexities and conflicts continue
to trouble student and teacher communication even after the teacher rejects traditional practices and embraces alternative, progressive ones—this
is not recognized, does not influence their theorizations of student voice.
Workshop and critical pedagogy advocates seem to forget that teacher-
student interaction is truly a complicated business.

It's a complicated business that is passed over too quickly in critical
pedagogues' calls for the questioning of student voice in the classroom.
Anita and Ms. Meyer's story, in chapter 2, suggests that teachers can inad-
vertently confound student expression just in trying to affirm and support
students' explorations of meaningful content. What risks for student expression, then, accompany the questioning—no, let's use the term Giroux
(1986) sometimes uses—the interrogation of student voice by the teacher?

In their work on women's development of voice, self, and mind, Mary
Belenky, Blythe Clinchy, Nancy Goldberger, and Jill Tarule (1986) argue

that a "doubting" model of education may be "peculiarly inappropriate" for women, if not inappropriate for men as well. They write:

> On the whole, women found the experience of being doubted debilitating rather than energizing. . . . Because so many women are already consumed with self-doubt, doubts imposed from outside seem at best redundant and at worst destructive, confirming the women's own sense of themselves as inadequate knowers. (p. 228)

I should note that Belenky and her coauthors are not arguing for an uncritical stance in relation to the world or the way the world is represented in the voices of students, teachers, and books—they would have teachers and students examine critically their worlds together. They also do not explicitly name critical pedagogy as a doubting model of education. In fact, they draw on Freire (1970) in their critique of traditional schooling, and also explicitly link their alternative vision of pedagogy—what they call "connected teaching"—to Freire's notion of a "problem-posing education."

Still, I take their doubts about doubting as words of caution for critical educators intent on interrogating student voice in the classroom. One of the reasons that I am not surprised that Belenky et al. refer approvingly to Freire is that he takes pains to explore and name the sorts of teacher qualities and educational conditions that can lessen the risks for students of sharing and exposing their meanings and values to others. But the risks remain. Simply supporting student voice in classrooms may be hard enough to accomplish. Advocates of critical pedagogy ask teachers to support and question student expression. Rather than pushing classroom participants' thought and action forward to increasingly critical evaluations of their world, such questioning could encourage students to not speak their minds, or to look for the correct thing to say to please the teacher. At times, critical pedagogues seem overconfident that student voice will flourish in the face of questioning.

When we left Mrs. Dunphy and Jinx above, neither Jinx nor Mrs. Dunphy were flourishing. Jinx had endured criticisms of his RUN-ON SENTENCES and doubts that the "I" of his "I Believe" essay was really himself. Mrs. Dunphy was feeling uneasy, even annoyed with "this tall hooded-eyed Negro boy standing there so unnaturally still." She and Jinx were entangled in those "different and incompatible discourses" Gilbert (1994) warned us about, and Mrs. Dunphy is now a little worried that she has pushed too hard on Jinx. It's time for some repair work on their relationship as teacher and student, so she points to a way that Jinx's work can be redeemed and that he can receive the reward that she is sure he wants, and is hers to bestow.

Attend. She doesn't understand the inadequacy of the repair work she proposes, doesn't understand the distance between Jinx and herself, the conflict masked in the polite voice Jinx uses at school:

> He's about to turn away so Mrs. Dunphy says, relenting, "If you rewrite it, making corrections, I might raise the grade. I might make an exception, this time."
>
> Jinx mumbles, "Yes, ma'am."
>
> "Will you, then?"
>
> "Ma'am?"
>
> "Rewrite it, make corrections? Hand it back in again, by Monday?"
>
> Jinx slips the composition in his notebook. His heart is beating hard and steady, keeping him cool, Iceman style. He's thinking that once there's blood on your hands, blood cries out for blood, doesn't it? This white bitch on her fat girdled ass, looking up at him with a fond-familiar smile, as if she has the right.
>
> He says, "Yes, ma'am, thank you, ma'am, I sure will."
>
> And he does. And the grade is raised to B+.

I confess that the first time I read through this vignette about Jinx and Mrs. Dunphy, the last sentence—"And the grade is raised to B+"—almost made me whoop out loud with angry satisfaction. For it seems that Jinx wins in his struggle with Mrs. Dunphy over his paper. Not only does he get the B+, but we also get to see him tell off Mrs. Dunphy, even if only inside his head. Jinx doesn't give in to Mrs. Dunphy and her definition of the situation, and he doesn't let her win by acquiescing to the initial grade she gave him.

But upon reflection, we also know that revising must have cost him, that the decision and labor to change his paper to please Mrs. Dunphy—Mrs. Dunphy with the "fond-familiar smile" that she has no right to share with him—could not have been easy. In the rewriting of his paper, Jinx had to choose among conflicting meanings and desires, had to orient himself among the voices of teacher and student, male and female, black and white, among the voices of Iceman and Verlyn (the agent of his mother's hopes). We can almost hear Jinx's teeth grinding as he "fixes" his RUN-ON SENTENCES and makes the voice of the paper conform to the voice Mrs. Dunphy knows is *Jinx*.

This inner dialogue and struggle, then, is the third kind of conflict (along with conflict among peers and between teacher and student) that workshop and critical pedagogy advocates have not confronted in their writing on student voice. Workshop advocates recognize that the writer faces difficulties in capturing complex experiences in words, difficulties in finding outer words to express inner meanings. But their conceptions of self and writing make it difficult to address the inner conflicts that attend having to use *others'* words, when those others are different from, opposed to, and more powerful than you. Bakhtin (1981) noted that

> Not all words for just anyone submit easily to this appropriation, to this sei-zure and transformation into private property: many words stubbornly re-sist, others remain alien, sound foreign in the mouth of the one who appro-priated them and who now speaks them . . . it is as if they put themselves in quotation marks against the will of the speaker. (p. 294)

Stephan Daedalus, the young Irish protagonist of James Joyce's (1916/1976) *A Portrait of the Artist as a Young Man*, expressed it this way, in his inner reflections on a conversation he was having with an English priest (who was also a dean at his school). Their discussion was moving, some-what haphazardly, through questions of esthetic theory and how to light fires and lamps, when the two discovered that they used a different word to name the same object—Stephan called the priest's "funnel" a "tundish." The priest, with a courtesy that Stephan thought rang false, called tundish "a most interesting word" and repeated it several times to himself. For Stephan, this "little word seemed to have turned a rapier point of his sen-sitiveness against this courteous and vigilant foe," the priest. Although both Stephan and the priest spoke English—as did Jinx and Mrs. Dunphy—Daedalus believed that

> The language in which we are speaking is his before it is mine. How differ-ent are the words *home, Christ, ale, master,* on his lips and mine! I cannot speak or write these words without unrest of spirit. His language, so familiar and so foreign, will always be for me an acquired speech. I have not made or accepted its words. My voice holds them at bay. My soul frets in the shadow of his language. (p. 189)[9]

Advocates of critical pedagogy, with their assumption of a multiple, social self, certainly are in better position than workshop advocates to recog-nize the inner struggles of Jinx and Stephan. When Giroux (1991) writes that one's voice "constitutes forms of subjectivity that are multilayered, mobile, complex, and shifting" (p. 100), he is pointing to a conception of voice that is not far from acknowledging inner conflict in the production of speech and writing in schools. Unfortunately, critical pedagogues have not usually pushed this far. Their conception of voice, as Elizabeth Ellsworth (1989) notes,

Does not confront the ways in which any individual student's voice is already a "teeth gritting" and often contradictory intersection of voices constituted by gender, race, class, ability, ethnicity, sexual orientation, or ideology. . . . It is impossible to speak from all voices at once, or from any one, without traces of the others being present and interruptive. (p. 312)

Before I close this section, I should interpret the references to "blood on your hands" and "blood cries out for blood" that interrupted Jinx's inner musings, above, as he considered the smiling Mrs. Dunphy who sat before him. What you don't know if you haven't read Oates's novel—and what Mrs. Dunphy never knows—is that Jinx is struggling with "Human Conscience" in his "I Believe" essay because he has killed someone.

Jinx killed "Little Red" Garlock, a white boy about Jinx's age. Jinx killed him partly in self-defense; partly in defense of a white girl, Iris, whom Jinx had befriended; partly because things never quite work out the way you expect them to. The fact that Jinx might be considered *innocent* of murder— innocent in legal and moral senses of the word—does not mean that Jinx considers himself so. This is part of his inner struggle.

Another part is that he doesn't feel that he can share what has happened with anyone other than Iris, who was a witness to the brutal fight within which Little Red was killed; and he is cut off even from Iris because of societal norms proscribing association between Blacks and Whites. He wants to tell his parents, but fears the hurt he will cause in the telling, and also fears that they will make him tell the police. As a young black male, he knows his dreams, his parents' dreams, of a college education will never be realized if he tells.

Little Red Garlock was loathed by Whites and Blacks alike—after he dropped out of school, he liked to roam the streets on his bicycle, calling out sexual obscenities to women and girls, looking for opportunities to bully. He came from a poor, wretched family. Figuring out how Little Red had ended up dead in the river was not a high priority to the police, and Jinx was never really at risk of being found out. But the burden of what had happened was heavy, and Jinx sometimes imagined confessing to the police:

At the police station, they'll take him into an interrogation room. They'll ask questions; he'll answer. His voice slow and hollow-sounding as it has been lately, in school. As if his voice isn't inside him but being thrown across a distance. As if he's a ventriloquist's dummy. (p. 196)

Police stations and classrooms are linked in Jinx's consciousness. Both represent white authority—an authority that will, if possible, determine his fate with little need of reference to the truth, what is right, or Jinx's own dreams.

I should take care here. I am not arguing that classrooms and police stations necessarily are or have to be linked for students who, like Jinx, find no easy place within the dominant meanings and values of society. Classrooms can be better places, learning places. Many already are such places, spaces where—through the hard work of teachers and students—students speak with voices not slow and hollow-sounding, but quick and resonant.

Classrooms can be better places, and we have a moral obligation, as educators, to make them so. But just because we are working to make them better doesn't mean that students don't confront problems in expressing themselves in classrooms, problems originating in conflicts with peers and teachers, in difficult choices of who they will be in relation to school and a larger, heterogeneous social world. I am not trying to be a glass-half-empty person. I am arguing that if our ideas of something better are linked to the flourishing of student voice in classrooms, then our theorizing and efforts to make things better have to account for the risks and problems students face in expressing themselves there.

Perhaps in a better world than Oates's novel—in a better world than we live in now?—Jinx could have told his story to Mrs. Dunphy and the police, and expected to be understood and treated fairly. But that's not the world he lived in, not the world he wrote in.

VOICE AS PROJECT

It is strange. Advocates of writing workshops and critical pedagogy are profoundly dissatisfied with the status quo. They want our ideas of writing and education, our teaching and learning in schools, our society, to move, change, grow, transform into something better. And yet their work portrays student voice as surprisingly static, undeveloping. In part, this problem can be understood with reference to the above criticism of their work: A sense of student voice as dynamic or in-process can be lost when the complexities, the struggles, the pushes and pulls of actually speaking and writing in classrooms are ignored. But student voice is rendered inert within the writings of workshop and critical pedagogy advocates for other reasons as well.

For workshop advocates, voice is the authentic expression of a stable, preexisting (Enlightenment) self. From this perspective, a student writer may need to look for, *discover*, her voice in her drafting and revision of texts, but her voice (like her self) is always already there, always already finished.

Thus, while individual texts may be constructed or developed, there is little sense of the student's voice undergoing construction or development—voice is *found*, not created.[10]

I argued that student voice was a starting point within the pedagogical scheme of critical pedagogues. Consequently, advocates of critical pedagogy pay quite a bit of attention to the contributions that student voice can make to critical, collective work in the classroom. But they do not attend to what this critical work means for the transformation of individual student voices. In other words, critical pedagogues may sketch how a student's story becomes the basis of a critical dialogue among teacher and students. Their focus on voice as starting point, however, leads to the neglect of how this critical dialogue then impacts the development of that student's voice. Within the writings of critical pedagogues, student voice remains frozen at the beginning of the educational process.

We need a revised, alternative conception of student voice—one that affirms workshop and critical pedagogy commitments to student expression and participation, but also helps us see student voice as in-process and embedded, for better and for worse, within the immediate social context of the classroom. I propose that voice be conceived of as a project involving *appropriation, social struggle,* and *becoming.* Before discussing each of these aspects, a few words on why I am proposing that we think of voice as a project.

A project takes time, has duration. So voice, here, is not construed as already finished or frozen, but as developing across time and situation. I would extend the prominent workshop images of writing as a craft or process to voice; that is, imagine our voices as something we can craft, as something we can develop with work.

A project suggests material to be worked, stuff to be manipulated. Voice as project resonates, then, with critical pedagogues' calls for a transformed recitation in which student contributions are grabbed hold of by the classroom community and shaken for integrity. Critical pedagogues, however, only help us imagine collective work on student voice. We also need to be able to make sense of and support individual projects, individual students working and reworking the stuff of their lives.

Finally, "project" has something of the smell and feel of school to it, the sense of a task or problem *taken up by actual students* as part of their everyday schoolwork. Imagining voice as a project, then, might help us keep our thinking about voice closer to the ground, closer to the struggles, victories, failures, of Jinx and Stephan and Anita and Jessie as they respond to the challenges and possibilities of complex social situations in the classroom. At the same time, construing voice as a project reaffirms the activity, the agency, of student writers in the production of their voices.

This is perhaps the strongest connection of my alternative conception of voice to those of critical pedagogy and workshop advocates. In the end, these advocates use the idea of voice to signal and call for the active presence of students in their own educations. Same here.

Appropriation

We begin with the social self sketched above and assumed by critical pedagogues—a multiple, in-process self created with the cultural resources made available by a complex social environment. My conception of voice is concerned with the speaking and writing of this emerging self, especially in schools.[11]

The notion of appropriation emphasizes the activity of the self in the face of cultural resources. That is, the concrete individual does not stand passive before the experiences, languages, histories, and stories that confront her, but assimilates and does work on these resources in crafting a self and a voice. In crafting her voice, the individual responds to and transforms the utterances of others in the production of her own speaking and writing. Thus, on the one hand, the idea of appropriation reminds us that our voices are dependent on the voices of others who preceded us and provided us with words to use. George Kamberelis and Karla Scott (1992) write that

> As individuals experience the language of others through social interaction, they collect words, phrases, styles, and structures and integrate them, forming a new synthetic object which we might call their individuality as language users and social beings. . . . [This process] transforms social and cultural experiences, particularly conversational experiences, into traces which live on in individual people, contributing to their being and speaking forth whenever the individuals talk or write. (p. 369)

On the other hand, the notion of appropriation highlights the taking over, the working over, by individuals, of the language of others. As Bakhtin (1986) put it: "These words of others carry with them their own expression, their own evaluative tone, which we must assimilate, rework, and reaccentuate" (p. 89).

For example, in our examination of a story by one of my third graders (Lensmire & Beals, 1994), Diane Beals and I noted a number of appropriations from oral and written sources that the young writer, Suzanne, had made in writing her text. Suzanne named some of the characters in her story after classmates. From a novel she was reading, Suzanne appropriated other characters' names, several story lines, and important themes. Within her story, Suzanne had one of her characters call out rhyming lines from the story of the gingerbread man: "Run, run, as fast as you can . . ." And finally, she appropriated a potent word from the speech of the local peer culture, a word that Suzanne and classmates used to tease and ostracize Jessie and other classmates.

Suzanne's appropriations, however, were not simple mimicry or repetition. She adapted and reworked the words and voices of others for her own purposes. Thus, in Suzanne's story, the rhyme from the gingerbread man was altered, and was chanted not by the gingerbread man to the wolf hot on his cookie heels, but by a brother who was unmercifully teasing his sister:

> Run, run, run,
> As fast as you can,
> You can't catch me
> You're the Zit man.

Saying that someone had "zits" (slang for pimples or acne) or was a "zit face" was a common form of abuse among Suzanne's classmates. Thus, the "Zit man" of the brother's rhyme echoed oral teasing engaged in by Suzanne and others. But Suzanne also reworked and reevaluated the word "zits" in her appropriation of it. For within Suzanne's story, two important characters—the brother and sister's father, and their older sister—condemn the brother's teasing and his rhyme. In other words, Suzanne's own creations (characters she presents as intelligent and caring in her writing) questioned the sort of teasing that she and her peers effected orally with the term *zits*.

Suzanne appropriated words, character names, rhymes, story lines, and themes from oral and written sources. She made them her own by giving them her own spin, by adapting them to her own purposes. And in this work, she was engaged in the project of developing her own voice out of the voices of others.

The notion of appropriation helps us to imagine student voice and its development with a concreteness missing from critical pedagogy. It also transforms workshop images of writing and voice. Instead of the writer as one who fishes the depths of subjectivity for morsels worthy of presentation, here we may well imagine the writer as the fish itself, swimming in a rich soup of words, and becoming a bigger or smaller, a faster or slower, a more or less beautiful fish, through its options and choices of what to take into its mouth.

To conclude this section, I will appropriate Michel Foucault's (1984) discussion of the use of notebooks (*hypomnemata*), in antiquity, to care for and develop the self. For Foucault, these notebooks "constituted a material memory of things read, heard, or thought, thus offering these as an accumulated treasure for rereading and later meditation" (p. 364). He emphasized that although these were personal notebooks, their primary purpose was not to give an account of oneself, to confess to temptation and failure as part of a process of purification, as was the case in later Christian versions. The contrast Foucault draws between these later and earlier uses of notebooks is analogous to the contrast I would draw between a workshop conception of voice and my alternative:

> The point is not to pursue the indescribable, not to reveal the hidden, not to say the non-said, but, on the contrary, to collect the already-said, to reassemble that which one could hear or read, and this to an end which is nothing less than the constitution of oneself. (p. 365)

Social Struggle

The idea of appropriation certainly suggests that the project of voice involves work. As sketched above, however, it suppresses the emotional turmoil and moral complexity that can accompany speaking and writing, ignores Jinx Fairchild's teeth-gritting, forgets Stephan Daedalus fretting in the shadow of the priest's language. To appropriation, then, we add social struggle as an important aspect of the project of voice. I point to three sorts of struggles that confront students in the development of their voices, with the recognition that in any actual production of voice, these three may be of varying importance, may blur into one another, may not be so easily identified and separated out.

The first is the struggle to use something old to do something new.[12] That is, the struggle to invest words, phrases, styles, and structures that have been used before—the given of convention and tradition—with new meaning, a meaning that is adequate to the student's goals for expression and the demands of the particular speech or writing situation with which he is confronted. Michael Holquist (1990) evokes this struggle when he writes that

> As denizens of the logosphere, the sea of words in which we pass our lives, we are surrounded by forms that in themselves seek the condition of mere being-there, the sheer givenness of brute nature. In order to invest these forms with life and meaning, so that we may be understood and so that the work of the social world may continue, *we must all perforce become authors*. (p. 66)

For Holquist, to be an author means to struggle to breathe new life into the old words and forms surrounding us. However, we must also recognize the politics of this struggle to appropriate the given. For what if the given are alien or hostile words from powerful others? Are forms not easily appropriated for the purposes you would pursue, for the experience of the world you would share?

As a black writer in the United States in the late 1920s, James Weldon Johnson (1928/1992) considered *the given* a formidable challenge for black authors who wanted to engage both black and white audiences. Literature, Johnson argued—if it was to achieve any "verisimilitude and finality," any "convincing power"—had to be based on "more or less well-established conventions, upon ideas that have some roots in the general consciousness" (p. 94). But the rooted ideas, the well-established words about black people in white America, were unworthy, hostile stereotypes, were brute forms too limited for an expansive literate engagement with black history and experience:

> It would be proof of little less than supreme genius in a Negro poet for him to take one of the tragic characters of American Negro history—say Crispus Attucks or Nat Turner or Denmark Vesey—put heroic language in his mouth and have white America accept the work as authentic. American Negroes as heroes form no part of white America's concept of the race. Indeed, I question if three out of ten of the white Americans who will read these lines know anything of either Attucks, Turner or Vesey, although each of the three played a role in the history of the nation. The Aframerican poet might take an African chief or warrior, set him forth in heroic couplets or blank verse and present him to white America with infinitely greater chance of having his work accepted. (pp. 94, 95)

Similarly, Carolyn Heilbrun (1988) describes how the conventions of women's biographies and autobiographies have long denied women's anger and desires for power and control over their own lives. The autobiographies of women such as Jane Addams and Ida Tarbell, for example, contrast sharply with their own accounts of experiences in diaries and personal correspondence. In their autobiographies, the work and quests these women determinedly pursued are rendered as good fortune or happenstance: "Each woman set out to find her life's work, but the only script insisted that work discover and pursue her, like the conventional romantic lover" (p. 25). Part of the struggle for women writing their lives, then, has been the struggle to resist and transform an inherited script that suppresses aspects of women's passion and agency.

But to resist or transform the given is risky, as Jinx learned when he tried to breathe new life into the school essay by investing it with personal meaning. His conversation with Mrs. Dunphy reminded him (if he had ever forgotten) that he could not write his text just to please himself. The question confronting Jinx was the one confronting any speaker or writer who wants to communicate:

> The question (and it is a political question involving the mediation of authority) always must be: how much uniqueness can be smuggled into a formula without it becoming unrecognizable to others? (Holquist, 1990, p. 135)

Becoming unrecognizable is especially risky for students in school. For the consequences extend beyond the awkwardness or pain of not being understood, of your audience not comprehending your meaning. The risk is rejection. In his attempt to smuggle himself into the inherited script, Jinx was like women who risk being dismissed as shrill or strident or divisive when they report their anger, like the first grader who violates convention with wobbly letters and invented spellings. Given the pervasiveness of evaluation in schools and students' subordinate positions, the risk of "becoming unrecognizable" is also the risk of not being *recognized* as a competent, worthy student and human being. Sometimes simply being unconventional is enough.

The second social struggle confronting students in schools, then, is the struggle to please or satisfy their audience. Teachers are an obvious, prominent audience for students, but students often speak and write for other audiences as well, including their families and local community. And within the conferences and sharing times of writing workshops, within the "transformed recitations" of critical pedagogy, classmates also command attention.

In her story about a second grader named Sammy, Anne Dyson (1995) underscores some of the difficulties and complexities that students face in writing for multiple, diverse audiences. Sammy joined his class late in the year, and consequently worked hard to fit into already established groups of friends and play partners. One of the places he pursued his desire to belong was in Author's Theater—a teacher-sponsored event in the classroom in which children performed their classmates' stories under the direction of the child authors. Dyson traces how Sammy wrote a series of different sorts of superhero stories in an attempt to provide valued peers (especially two popular, white middle-class boys named Seth and Jonathon) with satisfying roles to perform in Author's Theater. After early appropriations of teenage ninja and Superman stories, Sammy settled into writing X-Men stories, which, as Dyson notes, "potentially yielded a large team of good guys. Indeed, these mutant humans, with fantastic powers, soon took over as the dominant superheroes during writing time" (p. 28).

But Sammy was not settled for long. In writing his stories, Sammy followed his male peers in denying satisfying roles to female classmates, and this despite the fact that the X-Men stories of comic books and TV cartoons include powerful X-Men women. In other words, Sammy pleased only certain members of his peer audience, and he did it by writing stories that reaffirmed traditional gender stereotypes and relations. Girls in Sammy's class objected publicly to his and other boys' stories, let Sammy know that they were not pleased with the roles he would have them play.

Sammy was confronted with hard choices, choices wrapped up with his identity as a black working-class second grade boy and his desire to be accepted (recognized) by his classmates. Would he continue to write for and in solidarity with Seth and Jonathon? What about Holly and Tina, two black working-class girls from his neighborhood? They wanted good roles. Did he want to deny his common ground with them and deny them agency in his stories? Could he somehow please both boys and girls in his class, given their seemingly conflicting ideological positions on gender roles and relations?

Sammy's experiences point to the third social struggle students encounter in pursuing the project of voice in the classroom: the struggle to choose. Student speakers and writers are confronted with multiple voices expressing multiple and sometimes conflicting perspectives on the world. They are confronted with multiple audiences making multiple and sometimes conflicting demands. In the appropriation of certain voices (and not others), and in the particular ways they rework these voices, students position themselves with and against certain meanings and values, with and against certain audiences, in a social setting marked by asymmetries of power. Thus, the central challenge that Bakhtin (1984a) claimed confronts the heroes of Dostoevsky's novels, also confronts our students:

> All that matters is the choice, the resolution of the question "Who am I" and "With whom am I?" To find one's own voice and to orient it among other voices, to combine it with some and to oppose it to others, to separate one's voice from another voice with which it has inseparably merged—these are the tasks that the heroes solve in the course of the novel. (p. 239)

In the course of her study, Dyson's (1995) classroom hero, Sammy, gradually worked to separate his voice somewhat from those of his male peers, and created superhero stories with good roles for girls in his class. Indeed, he eventually described the characters in his stories not as X-Men, but as "X-people" (p. 34).

Still, any choice means saying no to other choices. And we must not underestimate the difficulty, risk, and pain that can accompany saying no to powerful voices and audiences.

If Foucault (surprisingly) helped me end the previous section on a rather upbeat note, I intone Karl Marx to close this section on social struggle.

In his preface to the first German edition of *Capital*, Marx (1867/1978) chided fellow Germans who comforted themselves with the belief that, because Germany was less developed industrially, it avoided the worst of the modern evils of capitalist production, as evidenced in England. Marx countered that not only did Germany have plenty of modern evils, but it was also plagued by a "whole series of inherited evils . . . arising from the passive survival of antiquated modes of production, with their inevitable train of social and political anachronisms" (p. 296).

In their speaking and writing, students strive to satisfy multiple, living audiences who reward and punish their efforts. They also struggle with a complex language inheritance, struggle to choose among and to redirect old words to new meanings. Students may well agree with Marx: "We suffer not only from the living, but from the dead."

Becoming

My account of voice-as-project has progressed peculiarly. My discussion of the social struggles students confront in producing voice made a problem out of what I had just said was the very way that students' voices develop. That is, appropriation, as the creation of one's own language out of the words of others, became the occasion for difficulty and strife.

We move peculiarly again, here, in order to recast the role of social struggle in the project of voice—not to forget its dangers, but to recognize its possibilities. For the very struggles that put the project of voice at risk are also the very possibility for growth and change. The new arises out of the struggle with the old, out of the struggle to please self and other, out of the struggle to stand with and against others and their words. To appropriation and social struggle, then, we add *becoming* as an important aspect of my conception of student voice.

What does the addition of becoming entail?

First, a recognition that there are no guarantees. The development of voice can, has, and will go in directions other than becoming. In other words, if becoming suggests an opening up of student voices, it also points to the possibility that they can be shut down. They can be shut down when students are overwhelmed by the inadequacy of the available or required forms of expression, despair at bridging the gap between old and new (O'Connor, 1989). They can be shut down when students refuse to speak or write in the face of hostile audiences and official voices, perhaps out of confusion and fear, but also out of dissent and anger—a silence grown out of a "deeply felt rage at those who live their unexamined privilege as entitlement" (Lewis, 1993, p. 3). Student voices can be shut down, as well, when students refuse to pay attention to other voices (if Sammy plugs his ears in response to Holly and Tina) and their voices harden and calcify, as habit (and not struggle) determines choice.

Second, making becoming part of the project of voice means that students and teachers are choosing, are valuing, what Dewey (1938) called growth or the reconstruction of experience; that is, the continual movement to "experiences of a deeper and more expansive quality" (p. 47). In terms of the project of voice, we might characterize becoming as the refusal, in our speaking and writing, to merely repeat the old. Instead, we are aiming for the reconstruction of the old—old words, old relations with audiences, old choices—in the service of the ongoing renewal of our perspectives on the world and our places within it. Becoming points to taking a position in relation to others and the meanings and values that precede us, but it also points to revising that position, that voice, across time.

Finally, the inclusion of becoming in our conception of voice entails the recognition that students cannot do it all by themselves. Students may be plagued by the living and the dead, but they need both if their voices are to continue developing. There is no way to fashion the new without the appropriation of the old. There is no opportunity for affirmation from your audience and the energy of collaboration without the risk of rejection. And there is no chance to become who you want to become, to speak with a voice that is yours—even as that voice sounds with the voices of others with whom you've learned and struggled—without the pain that often accompanies saying *this*, and not *that*. Students need others if their voices are to continue to develop. Within the classroom, they need teachers who recognize their struggles for voice, and help them transform these struggles into occasions for becoming.[13]

In the end, committing ourselves to becoming is committing ourselves to a view of what it means to be human. It is to align ourselves with Dewey's belief that humanity is

> A participant in an unfinished universe rather than a spectator of a finished one. In order to survive and exalt our existence, we must creatively solve our problems and evolve life-affirming values, perhaps of a kind that have never before existed. (Garrison, 1995, p. 418)

Bakhtin says somewhere that to be is to communicate (actually, he probably says this everywhere). And to communicate is to struggle to speak and write in ways that somehow answer to the unique demands of unique situations that have never occurred before. In other words, Bakhtin saw demands for becoming in our everyday existence, saw struggle and creativity as facts of life.

In Charles Dickens's novel *A Christmas Carol*, an old Scrooge looked back with joy at his employment under a man named Fezziwig. It was not that the work that Scrooge and his colaborers performed was easy—the work was very hard and toilsome. But in Fezziwig's treatment of Scrooge and the others, in his way of being with them, Scrooge thought that Fezziwig had the power to make the work heavy or light—and Fezziwig made it light.

The project of voice is hard. Appropriation, social struggle, and becoming demand labor, risk-taking, and imagination. The challenge for those of us who would have student voices flourish in schools is to extend the work of writing workshop and critical pedagogy advocates, and continue to find better ways of being with students—ways that make the unavoidable burdens of voice light.

A CONCLUSION

One of the last times we see Jinx Fairchild in *Because It Is Bitter, and Because It Is My Heart*, he is about to interact, again, with someone who works for an important institution of white authority. Jinx is 24 years old, married, searching for meaningful work (his shot at a college scholarship ended with a broken ankle in the final basketball game of his senior year). But this time, the person behind the desk is black. And when Jinx approaches, the person stands, embraces his hand. And to Jinx's surprise, the person even recognizes him, calls him by the name that celebrated his nerve, his power, on the basketball floor, the name he was known by when life seemed open:

> Birth certificate carefully folded in his inside jacket pocket, Jinx Fairchild takes the bus uptown on this Saturday morning in November 1963 to the United States Army recruiting station on South Main Street and first thing he sees, shyly entering the office, is that the smartly uniformed man behind the counter, seated at a desk, is black . . . which he hadn't envisioned.
>
> At once he's flooded with relief.
>
> Then the second amazing thing: this man Jinx Fairchild doesn't know, could swear he has never laid eyes on before, strong-boned handsome face, skin dark as Jinx's own, a man in his mid-thirties at least, is evidently from Hammond, for it seems he knows Jinx, or recognizes him: rising quickly to his feet, reaching across the counter to shake Jinx's hand, smiling, happy, deep booming voice: "*Iceman*—isn't it?" (p. 367)

Jinx was recognized, accepted, not by his teacher, but by his army recruiting officer. And he would lend the powers of his body, not the powers of his voice, to his country's project. November 1963—signing up then, the month Kennedy was killed, would give him enough time to get ready for Vietnam.

I conclude with a few lines from Cornel West's (1989) statement of what it is we might learn if we pay close attention to the voice of W.E.B. Du Bois. They are an appropriately hopeful and sobering conclusion to my meditation:

> Creative powers reside among the wretched of the earth even in their subjugation, and the fragile structures of democracy in the world depend, in large part, on how these powers are ultimately exercised. (p. 148)

NOTES

1. Stanley Aronowitz (Aronowitz & Giroux, 1991), bell hooks (1989, 1994), and Peter McLaren (Giroux & McLaren, 1989; McLaren, 1994) have also been important for my understanding of voice and critical pedagogy. It seems that Giroux, however, has given the most explicit attention to the idea of voice among critical pedagogues, and, consequently, my characterization of voice in critical pedagogy here is based largely on his work. I should note that neither writing workshop nor critical pedagogy advocates write only about *student* voice—workshop advocates make no real distinction between voice for student writers and other writers; and critical pedagogues sometimes write of teacher and curriculum voices, in addition to student voice. And of course, other educators and researchers have written productively about voice—I draw on a number of them later in the chapter. See also Yancey's (1994) edited volume, *Voices on Voice.*

2. All quotations from Oates's novel, unless noted, come from this vignette (pp. 173–175).

3. I wonder what Mrs. Dunphy would say about her creator's writing, since Oates's novels are full of RUN-ON SENTENCES. One of my favorites, from *Foxfire: Confessions of a Girl Gang* (1994):

> Huron Radiator, Hammond's largest employer (as it was always boasting) had laid off one-fifth of its employees last year with the brazen intention of relocating some of its operations in West Virginia where nonunion workers could be hired, and there was a long bitter sporadically violent strike in effect against Ferris Plastics where Muriel used to work, we saw the strikers marching carrying their red-lettered A.F. OF L. STRIKE signs we saw their drawn faces, worried angry eyes the eyes of men and women who don't control their futures knowing FINANCES are the wormy heart of our civilization, can you live in dignity with such a truth? (p. 213)

4. For Berlin (1988), workshop advocates embrace an "expressionistic rhetoric" that is the descendant of both Rousseau and Romantic responses to nineteenth-century capitalism. This rhetoric assumes an autonomous, stable self who takes up relations with the world in order to make sense of it and herself, and is characterized by a radical individualism that portrays the individual as the

source and final arbiter of what *is*, of what is *good*, and of what is *possible*. It is not that the reality of material, social, and linguistic aspects of the world are denied, but that

> They are considered significant only insofar as they serve the needs of the individual. All fulfill their true function only when being exploited in the interests of locating the individual's authentic nature. (p. 484)

Expressionistic rhetoric's critique of society emerges from this demand that the material and social contexts of the individual support the pursuit and discovery of personal meaning. Berlin argues that this rhetoric has been closely tied to psychological theories that assert the inherent goodness of the individual, and that within expressionistic rhetoric, this inherent goodness is, of course, "distorted by excessive contact with others in groups and institutions" (p. 484)—social relations and institutions (such as schools) corrupt human nature and demand conformity to petty social convention, rather than provide the supportive backdrop for a flourishing individuality.

5. At first glance, it seems that Iceman might be the male Enlightenment ideal, until we remember that this ideal includes the opposition of mind and body. For Jinx, Iceman flourished on the basketball court, where Jinx's identity was "so much a matter of fluidity, sloping shoulders, elastic spine, sly head cocked to one side" (Oates, 1990, p. 403). But Iceman certainly seems related to "Cool Cat"—one of the character types Perkins describes in his *Home Is a Dirty Word: The Social Oppression of Black Children*:

> The Cool Cat often appears indifferent to the problems around him, as though he is insensitive to pain, frustration or death. He rarely allows his real inner feelings to surface. . . . The Street Institution has trained him to act in this manner, to be cool, stern, impersonal in the face of all kinds of adversities. (cited in Gilyard, 1991, p. 112)

6. Bakhtin uses "languages" to stand both for what he calls "national languages" such as Spanish or English, as well as dialects and "ways with words" (Heath, 1983) within a single national language.

7. I am simplifying a bit here, with the characterization of voice as endpoint in writing workshop and voice as starting point in critical pedagogy. Workshop advocates will sometimes talk of voice as a driving force or essential ingredient in the writing process itself (Graves, 1983). Thus, voice is linked not only to a quality of the text produced, but to the assumed natural desire to express the self. Within critical pedagogy, voice is sometimes used to suggest a desired endpoint in the development of the individual, as when Giroux (1988) calls for "a voice capable of speaking in one's own terms, a voice capable of listening, retelling, and challenging the very grounds of knowledge and power" (p. 71).

8. There are important exceptions—for example, Lewis and Simon (1986), Weiler (1988), and McLaren (1994). Work such as this leads to more complex renderings of pedagogy within work on critical pedagogy. But it doesn't seem that such work has led to serious revisions of the idea of student voice.

9. McDermott (1988) discusses this Joycean example of inner conflict over language in his wonderful piece on "Inarticulateness."

10. Gilbert (1989b) notes that even the crafting of texts and revision (especially in response to response from peers and teacher) are sometimes considered suspect by certain supporters of workshop approaches. Why? Because the expression of personal meaning is often linked to spontaneity—and calls for spontaneity don't necessarily go well with calls for revision and better communication with your audience.

11. I do not want to reduce the self to voice. I assume that voice is an aspect of the self, but not the whole self. I want to limit student voice to actual speaking and writing, even as this speaking and writing would certainly be seen as linked to and in interaction with other actions of the self (thinking, nonverbal communication, dancing, playing sports, etc.).

12. Wertsch (1991) writes about this struggle in terms of an inherent tension between, on the one hand, mediational means or impersonal tools, and on the other, the unique, personal uses to which these means are put.

13. A stunning example of this is provided by Soliday (1994) in her discussion of the use of literacy narratives to help college students make sense of their own paths into schooling and literacy. In terms of my discussion here, what is most important about Soliday's piece is its portrayal of students who, in the struggle to choose between the languages and identities brought from home and those demanded in schools, refused to resolve these tensions by choosing one or the other. That is, they rejected old choices and created new ones.

4

Community, Deliberation, and Transgressive Stories

How will the creative powers of children and young adults in schools be recognized and developed?

I explored writing workshop advocates' answer to this question in previous chapters. With the help of Mikhail Bakhtin's writings on carnival and Dostoevsky, I affirmed the free and familiar contacts among students and teachers and the playful relation to the world promoted by workshop advocates. I praised their rejection of monologism, their embrace of a plurality of student voices. I commended workshop advocates' vision of an alternative teacher position that asks teachers to help students live and write about their own vigorous, adventurous lives, inside and outside the classroom.

At the same time, I worried about how Jessie removed herself from the workshop's public spaces because she recognized no friends there; how Anita expressed herself to (hid her self from) a supportive, perceptive teacher (a superior who had her under surveillance). I criticized workshop advocates for ignoring social and cultural boundaries and hierarchies that animate children's lives within and without workshops, for remaining silent about the silencing effects of smaller and larger cultural politics of meaning. I objected to workshop advocates' overly individualistic and private conception of voice, and labored to express an alternative conception that would somehow do justice to how Jinx and Sammy labored to express their very souls on paper, with words not theirs, and anticipating the conflicting desires and demands of readers friendly and unfriendly, readers beside, below, above. I questioned the narrow, technical work imagined for teachers—work that abandons students to the current world, to dominant meanings and values, rather than engages students in deliberation about that world, in criticism and transgression of those meanings and values. Work that might actually help students move with power and responsibility, help them be free.

I like imagining workshops as carnival, and teachers as Dostoevskian novelists. I think these metaphors help us enrich and extend workshop approaches, even as they help us raise questions and name problems. In this chapter, I work through some problems that I have, so far, only named. I respond to three questions: How—after we recognize limits to carnival's abundance—do we imagine desirable classroom communities? If we desire deliberation about meanings and values in the workshop, what does such deliberation sound like? And if we are serious about helping students imagine and create new worlds to live in, how do we think about and support such transgression? I am obviously not the first to take up such questions; my responses are anything but exhaustive. I hope they will be helpful.

DESIRABLE CLASSROOM COMMUNITIES

I follow John Dewey (1916/1966), in his *Democracy and Education*, in my effort to imagine desirable, worthy classroom communities. Dewey argues that the education various communities provide is dependent on the quality or worthiness of those forms of life. We are confronted immediately, then, with the "need of a measure for the worth of any given mode of social life" (p. 83). In creating this measure or ideal, Dewey cautions, we must avoid two extremes. We cannot just make up our ideal "out of our heads"—if we do, we have little assurance that we can pull off or even approach it in practice. We also cannot simply name whatever already exists as our ideal.

Dewey's method for creating his "measure" and avoiding these extremes is to "extract the desirable traits of forms of community life which actually exist, and employ them to criticize undesirable features and suggest improvement" (p. 83). When he does this, Dewey arrives at two questions that we can use to assess the quality of community life. Before sharing these two questions, Dewey reminds us that any given community or society is actually always made up of a number of smaller communities or groups. Dewey's first question is concerned primarily with life within these smaller social groups, the second with interactions across these groups. So:

> Now in any social group whatever, even in a gang of thieves, we find some interest held in common, and we find a certain amount of interaction and cooperative intercourse with other groups. From these two traits we derive our standard. How numerous and varied are the interests which are consciously shared? How full and free is the interplay with other forms of association? (p. 83)

When Dewey uses these questions to judge the worthiness of the life and education afforded by his gang of thieves, he finds that (1) the interests shared are few—"reducible almost to a common interest in plunder"—and that (2) this interest serves to "isolate the group from other groups with respect to the give and take of the values of life." That is, the quality of the thieves' lives is diminished by the lack of a variety of activities and experiences that would develop and expand shared interests within the group, and by the lack of meaningful interactions with other groups—groups that represent (and present as opportunities for growth) alternative meanings and values. The education provided by such a group, Dewey concludes, is "partial and distorted" (p. 83).

In contrast, when Dewey applies his measure to a healthy family, he finds that (1) there are "material, intellectual, and aesthetic interests in which all participate and that the progress of one member has worth for the experience of other members" and that (2) the family is not isolated from other social groups, but "enters intimately into relationships with business groups, with schools, with all the agencies of culture" and "plays a due part in the political organization and in return receives support from it" (p. 83). Such a family does well against Dewey's standard—many interests are consciously shared and communicated, and the family enters into numerous contacts with other forms of association.

Below, I use Dewey's questions to evaluate writing workshops and make suggestions for their improvement as a form of associated living. Before I do this, however, I need to expand briefly upon one aspect of Dewey's analysis, as it is a key assumption in my evaluation.

Dewey emphasizes that within any given society or community there are always numerous smaller societies and communities. He evokes this pluralism with reference to political, industrial, scientific, and religious associations; political parties, cliques, gangs, corporations, and partnerships; and diverse populations with diverse languages, religions, morals, codes, and traditions. Dewey (1916/1966) writes that

> From this standpoint, many a minor political unit, one of our large cities, for example, is a congeries of loosely associated societies, rather than an inclusive and permeating community of action and thought. (p. 82)

In what follows, my "minor political unit" is the classroom—more specifically, the writing workshop. Furthermore, I assume that this workshop community is not some sort of tight, "inclusive and permeating community," but rather a collection of "loosely associated societies." I refer to these smaller societies within the workshop community as *friendship groups*, and use this phrase to evoke the myriad ways that children divide themselves up—sometimes for better and sometimes for worse, sometimes for an hour and sometimes for years—when given the chance.

One danger with imagining the workshop community as a collection of friendship groups is that it might exaggerate fragmentation, might make the walls that divide groups of children seem higher and sturdier than they are. Consequently, we might not pay attention to how children sometimes jump over and knock down walls, and we might miss possibilities for our practice and theory on how to help them do it.

I'll try to be careful. At the same time—and this should come as no surprise—I am equally concerned that writing workshop advocates, and progressive literacy educators and researchers in general, often ignore or wish away hierarchies and divisions among children.[1] With Dewey's help, then, I try to respect the lines children draw without necessarily accepting them once and for all.

Here goes.

I have argued that workshops enable students to participate actively in workshop life, to take up free and familiar relations with each other, and to take up playful, adventurous relations with the world. In other words— in the words of Dewey's first question—workshops allow children to express and share numerous and varied interests in each other and the world. I have said, and I say here, that this is good.

Because students in workshops are able to choose whom they will work with, they usually collaborate and conference within friendship groups. Students' interests, then, are not only expressed in their written texts, but also in their patterns of association in the workshop. The worst thing we can say about these texts and friendship groups, at this point, is that they might express *already formed* interests—interests formed in the meanings and values of the playground, family, neighborhood, and popular culture; formed in the workings of social class, gender, and race. But this isn't much of a criticism—yet. *We all come from somewhere.* Furthermore, the techniques taught in workshops about how to compose and revise texts and how to respond to peers *do help* students develop their texts and work with each other more effectively. Workshops are good for allowing children to associate in friendship groups, and they help children work more effectively within these groups.

Thus, workshops do well with the first question of Dewey's test.

They fail the second.

We can characterize this failure in terms of the quantity and quality of interplay among friendship groups in writing workshops.

I reported in chapter 1 how students in a third grade workshop divided themselves up along social class and gender lines, and how they avoided contact with students on the other side of those lines. Friendship groups tended to cut themselves off from interactions with other groups. When they came into contact—when children's "forms of association" came into "interplay" with each other—it was not necessarily in ways that led to sharing and hearing and learning. Instead, this interplay was often characterized by distrust and hostility and competition, and served to reassert hierarchies and boundaries, rather than blur or transgress them. Friendship groups may have been friendly on the inside, but not in their relations to other groups.

My argument does not depend on children and friendship groups in every workshop, everywhere, conducting themselves exactly like this one. However, I do assume that adults and children make distinctions about who and what they find more and less desirable. Furthermore, I assume that these distinctions have consequences for our actions, consequences for our choices of whom we will associate with and for the talk and texts we produce. These distinctions can change—certainly, hopefully. But at any given moment, choices are made and have effects in the world. My claim about workshops, then, is simply this: *Nothing* about student choice *assures communication across friendship groups.*[2]

What about sharing time, when student authors sit in the front of the room and read their work to the class? This seems the perfect occasion for the interplay of friendship groups in the workshop, a time when the voices of diverse forms of life would sound and be answered within the larger public, the classroom community. When we listen to how sharing time is orchestrated by workshop advocates, however, we are disappointed (if not surprised) by its thin, narrow range. For sharing time is arranged the same as teacher response to text—affirm the writer, discuss technique. A plurality of student groups might express themselves in the stories read, but their meanings and values, their imaginative visions, are ignored, disregarded in the pursuit of "what works and what needs work" (Murray, 1985, p. 140).

My treatment of deliberation, below, is aimed exactly at supporting an alternative sort of sharing time, one that might redeem workshop approaches in relation to Dewey's ideal. But first I must address—and reject—an obvious solution to this problem of limited interaction among students from different friendship groups.

Make them work together. Regulate collaboration and peer conferences with a nod, perhaps, to cooperative learning group schemes in which the teacher intervenes directly in decisions of whom children will associate and work with in the classroom. After all, why should we allow students to choose whom they will work with when these choices often reproduce divisions by race and gender and social class that we hope to undermine? In grander language: Are we not supporting an unworthy sort of pluralism—separatism—in our support of student-chosen friendship groups in the workshop community?

Dewey (1916/1966) certainly rejects separatism:

> The essential point is that isolation makes for rigidity and formal institution-
> alizing of life, for static and selfish ideals within the group. . . . It is a com-
> monplace that an alert and expanding mental life depends upon an enlarg-
> ing range of contact with the physical environment. But the principle applies
> even more significantly to the field where we are apt to ignore it—the sphere
> of social contacts. (p. 86)

If a group remains isolated, it is denied the chance to grow, to become more
flexible. When we interact with others outside our primary associations,
we encounter different ways of acting, thinking, and feeling. These provide opportunities for us to expand and reflect upon and reconstruct our
own habits, our own characteristic ways of being in the world.

And of course, the problem is not just one of isolation. Hierarchies of
influence and assumed value usually accompany separation:

> The influences which educate some into masters, educate others into slaves
> . . . The more activity is restricted to a few definite lines—as it is when there
> are rigid class lines preventing adequate interplay of experiences—the more
> action tends to become routine on the part of the class at a disadvantage . . .
> The evils thereby affecting the superior class are less material and less per-
> ceptible, but equally real. Their culture tends to be sterile, to be turned back
> to feed on itself; their art becomes a showy display and artificial; their wealth
> luxurious; their knowledge overspecialized; their manners fastidious rather
> than humane. (pp. 84, 85)

I love how Dewey gives it to privileged groups here (I would say from close
observation and depressing experience in the university that he's got it
about right)—this is especially fun because members of these groups are
his most likely readers.

However, I am troubled by how we might interpret Dewey's account
of the dangers of separation and hierarchy for subjugated groups, and by
what this interpretation suggests for their struggle to survive and to contest
this subjugation. At times, Dewey seems to frame the problem as one of
quantity (consider his call for "numerous" shared interests as part of his
"measure" or "standard"[3]). That is, what oppressed groups really need is
more interaction with other, including privileged, groups. If we frame the
problem this way, then it would *never be reasonable* for members of these
groups *to limit their interactions* with others. *More interplay, more learning, more
good.* Cooperative learning groups—in which teachers purposefully assign
diverse students to groups in ways that put diverse strengths into play in
problem solving and task completion—are built on just this sort of thinking.

In the end, Dewey is concerned with both quantity and quality of interaction. My concern, however, is not a better interpretation of Dewey, but this: that we remember that harm is accomplished not just through isolation, not just through *no contact*, but also *in contact, in interaction with other groups*. More interaction can mean more opportunity for injury, more opportunity to be watched and controlled. If this is true, then it becomes *very reasonable* for members of subjugated groups to, at times, *purposefully limit interaction with other groups*.

What does this have to do with friendship groups in the writing workshop? I want to interpret and defend friendship groups—and their seemingly separatist ways—as reasonable, as embryonic forms of what Patricia Hill Collins (1991), in her exploration of black women's activism, calls group survival and community-building.[4]

Collins conceptualizes black women's activism along two primary dimensions: (1) the struggle for group survival and community-building, and (2) the struggle for institutional transformation. In her portrayal of the struggle for group survival, she pays particular attention to black women's efforts to create "Black female spheres of influence" within which alternative patterns of consciousness, self-expression, and value, to those of dominant groups, are nurtured and developed. For Collins, these spaces represent "Black women's refusal to relinquish control over their self-definition" to a dominant ideology that defines them as mule, mammy, Jezebel, and welfare mother (p. 142). This sense of refusal, and the need for time and place for the hard work of alternative vision, is evident in the words of black civil rights activist and musician Bernice Johnson Reagon. Reagon evokes the sound and feel of a conversation in a "little barred room" safe from intrusions by the outer world:

> That space while it lasts should be a nurturing space where you might sift out what people are saying about you and decide who you really are ... in that little barred room where you check everybody at the door, you act out community. You pretend that your room is a world. (cited in Collins, 1991, p. 145)

Collins emphasizes that the struggle for group survival and community building is not enough, that struggle for institutional transformation is also essential. But she is careful to emphasize that the two are related, and not just in the sense that a given, concrete action may contribute to both struggles at once. These struggles are related in the sense that they represent different moments in a larger, continuous effort to bring about social change. Thus, for Collins,

> Group survival is designed to foster autonomy . . . [and] autonomy provides
> the foundation for principled coalition with other groups that are essential
> for institutional transformation. (p. 145)

In other words, action that fosters autonomy, that sustains and strength-
ens a subordinated community, creates possibilities for that group to come
together with other groups in ways that might benefit everyone.

This is my defense of friendship groups: that students, especially students not aligned with and maligned by dominant meanings and values,
need them. Students need them as safe (or at least safer) spaces of self-
definition and resistance, need them to construct platforms from which to
speak with autonomy. Let them enact community away from hostile peers
and the teacher's surveilling eyes; let them pretend that their barred room
is the world. *For the moment.* For the moment it takes to name the world
and their places in it, in writing.

Collins (1991) rejects interpretations of black women's activism that
would reduce it either to this or that—as aimed at *either* group survival *or*
institutional transformation, as expressing *either* a form of separatism *or* a
vision of racial integration. Instead, Collins argues that this tradition of
activism embodies a "both/and humanist vision of society" that has space
for *both* group survival *and* institutional transformation as worthy, has time
for different strategies required at different times (p. 161).

Dewey's ideal, of course, had a both/and logic from the beginning.
His ideal society is not one that depends on squeezing and flattening out
plurality into a single, tight, permeating community that must look like this
or that. Instead, his ideal values shared *both* meanings and interests within
groups *and* the interplay and conflict of these meanings and interests as
different groups interact. Dewey, of course, wants the conflict of different
groups played out in a way that is conducive to listening, learning, and
reconstruction. So do I.

I embrace a both/and interpretation of friendship groups, and reject interpretations that would pronounce them either good or bad. They
are both—and their ultimate worth, in this case, depends on what happens in another workshop moment: sharing time. We recognize friendship groups while at the same time working to keep them as fluid as
possible. We grant students the right to make distinctions, to choose who
they need for comfort, courage, information, and inspiration. But we also
create public spaces, sharing times, within which the meanings and
values issuing from these student-chosen groups—and even the internal
workings of them—are questioned, shaken for integrity, deliberated, and
reconstructed.

One final both/and. Now that I have argued as best I can for allowing students to choose and work within friendship groups in the writing workshop, and have rejected cooperative learning groups as a solution to the problem of limited interaction among different groups of students, I confess *both* that I have, as an elementary, junior high, and university teacher, assigned students to cooperative learning groups in the past *and* that I will in the future. Student-chosen groups are an extremely important aspect of my own teaching. They are accompanied by explicit talk about the benefits and risks for self and community of choosing differently next time, as well as, occasionally, by more direct teacher intervention into patterns of student association. In the end, teacher judgement, not this or that argument, must carry the day. My purpose is not to restrict teacher action, especially in the form of a once-and-for-all proscription of cooperative learning groups. Instead, I have defended friendship groups because student autonomy—including students' primary associations—should not be disregarded without pause, without careful reflection.

DELIBERATION AND STORIES

A melody is a chord deployed in time. (Dewey, 1934/1989, p. 189)

I have been haunted by this line from Dewey's *Art as Experience* for some time. It conjures Dr. Borowitz, I suppose, and the music theory and composition tricks he taught me almost two decades ago in college. (If you are trying to make up a melody, for example, you can start with a chord and simply play the notes that make it up one after the other—literally "deploying" the chord "in time.") But I think Dewey's line haunts my thoughts more for how it expresses, in such condensed form, the unity of space and time in our experience of art and life.

The line concludes Dewey's argument against conceiving of some arts as spatial and others as temporal. Instead, Dewey asserts, space and time are "common to the substance of all works of art" (p. 210). Painting, for example, is considered a spatial art. But in our experience of a painting, our attention shifts, moves, from place to place, from this aspect to that. This doesn't happen in an instant; the earlier influences the later. Our experience of painting, then, depends on movement not only through space but through time.

We readily recognize this movement in music—music doesn't exist without time for its sounds to unfold, without time to play itself out. Dewey reminds us, however, that the sounds of music shrink, expand, rise, fall;

that tones are "high and low, long and short, thin and massive" (p. 213). He reminds us that space is crucial to music, that we "*hear* distances and volumes in music" in the intervals between notes in a melody and the piling up of sounds on top of one another in chords and harmonies (p. 188).

My sketch of desirable classroom communities in the last section emphasized space in our own and students' experience of the writing workshop. Friendship groups drew lines; they were isolated and distant from or in contact with other groups; they sought safe places behind doors, walls. Friendship groups were piled up—in hierarchies of power and value—like notes in a chord.

It's time, then, to emphasize time, to pay attention to how the relations among friendship groups might play themselves out, unfold. I attend to two particular times in the workshop: to how the relations of friendship groups play out in sharing time, and to how these relations unfold in the stories students write.

Let's begin again.

A story is a world deployed in time. (me, now, here)

I have criticized workshop sharing times because they allow the worlds deployed by students' stories to be extended without discussion about whether or not these are the worlds within which students and we want to live. I am especially concerned about the social worlds deployed by student stories—how these stories contribute to the ongoing face-to-face relations among individuals and friendship groups in the workshop, and how students' stories reach outside the workshop to grab larger patterns of relation and meaning and value, and then hold them up, during sharing time, as ways to be with each other in the world.

Stories give us, among other things, *direction*. Direction works for and on us in two ways. It works by *focusing* our attention and action on certain things and not others: "Look there! Isn't that a beautiful bird?" And it works by *ordering* our activity, by calling out certain actions at certain moments: "Duck! Too late—oh, that's going to leave a mark."[5] Stories provide direction; they focus and order our responses to the world. Or, as J. Hillis Miller (1995) puts it: Stories are "policemen of culture" (p. 69).

Workshop advocates ask teachers to support the direction of students' stories without asking them to consider—and without asking students to consider—where these stories lead. I propose, then, *deliberation* about stories in sharing time. I mean deliberation in Dewey's (1922) sense of a "dramatic rehearsal (in imagination) of various competing lines of action" (p. 190). For Dewey, deliberation is a playing out, a rehearsal, of what would happen if we pursued this or that path. During this rehearsal, we pay close attention to our own and others' responses to the action. Deliberation is dramatic—both in the sense that it involves unfolding scenarios and in the sense that it is emotionally charged (Caspary, 1991). Dewey emphasized that deliberation is not some dry projection of profit or pleasure or pain. Instead, deliberation involves a full-bodied (if vicarious) experience of this and that course of action. Not only do we try to see our way, we try to feel it:

> To every shade of imagined circumstance there is a vibrating response; and to every complex situation a sensitiveness as to its integrity, a feeling of whether it does justice to all facts, or overrides some to the advantage of others. Decision is reasonable when deliberation is so conducted. (Dewey, 1922, p. 194)

When a student writes a story, she is engaged in the imaginative rehearsal of possible lines of action. She is engaged in deliberation.[6] Deliberation is also enacted within friendship groups, when friends mark more than run-on sentences, mark the desirability of deployed worlds. In what follows, however, I use deliberation to name what happens—what we hope happens—*after* students' stories have been shared, made public, within the workshop.[7]

Patricia Clifford, Sharon Friesen, and David Jardine (1995) remind us of what we *do not want* to have happen. They focus our attention on a story written by a primary school student named Sinead and explore what it might teach us about living, literacy, and schooling. Sinead's story is about a Christmas concert disrupted by a howling coyote. However, Clifford, Friesen, and Jardine demonstrate how Sinead's story is *also* a profound and generous re-writing of the identity and place of one of her classmates, Manuel. Manuel was the object of psychological testing and school practices (what Clifford, Friesen, and Jardine call "uppercase events like Attention Deficit Disorder, Hyperactivity, Learning Disabilities, Developmental Delays") that certified him defective and banished him to the margins of classroom and school communities (p. 15). With the help of the native trickster figure, Coyote, Sinead challenged these official school pronouncements and placements; in her story, "Manuel the monster child is welcomed in from the margins and given a home" (p. 9).

Clifford, Friesen, and Jardine show how Sinead's is a value-and meaning-*full* story. Their exasperation and sense of injustice are apparent when they imagine the technical, empty response this story would receive if teachers and students performed, in sharing time, as directed by workshop advocates:

> "That's nice, Sinead. Thank you for sharing your story with us," someone might have said as they plunked her into the Author's Chair (Calkins, 1986) and unleashed a barrage of profound illiteracies:

"How long did it take you to write?"
"Where did you get your ideas from?"
"I like the part with the howling. What part did *you* like best?" (p. 17)

Deliberation changes what students' stories are in the classroom community. Instead of mindless direction, students' stories represent mind-full experiments of how we might live, testable hypotheses of better and worse ways to quickly and slowly wind and unwind our legs, arms, hands, in space and time. As a first move in deliberation, a story is

A form of inquiry that can contain both the world and the relations within which it becomes the focus of our attention . . . Like our bodies, it literally takes place. Its storyline takes up time, as we do, from beginning to end. (Grumet, 1990, p. 107)

Sharing Time

Sharing times characterized by deliberation among members of different friendship groups—the "full and free interplay" of Dewey's ideal—demand certain virtues of workshop participants and expose them to certain dangers. My account of these virtues and dangers is brief, and draws on Richard Bernstein's (1992) work in *The New Constellation*. First, I name several responsibilities that students need to take up in their interaction with other students about stories. Then I list four dangers lurking in deliberation, even as students try to act virtuously in relation to each other. I close by returning to a problem first raised in chapter 2—the problem of the teacher's role in writing workshops. I compile a medley of teacher responsibilities—responsibilities called out by and answering to the responsibilities and dangers of deliberation for students.

Students' first responsibility in sharing time is to *listen carefully* to the stories and comments of others. Such listening depends on the assumption by students that their peers—including those in other friendship groups—have something to say, and that this something might contribute to their understanding of themselves and the world. Workshop advocates want students to listen to others' stories during sharing time. They provide concrete suggestions for how to help students listen and respond to peers' work. This listening and response are aimed at improving the effectiveness of the author's writing processes and text. Thus, students are supposed to assume that their peers are writers and can improve *how* they write—this is good. However, there is no demand that students attend and respond to *what* is said, the meanings and values, the direction, expressed by stories.

This demand *is* present in the literacy practices described by Patricia Enciso and Bronwyn Davies. Enciso (1992, 1996) focuses on how we might help young children articulate their experiences of stories. In what Enciso calls "symbolic representation interviews," children created paper cutouts that represented a story's characters, setting, and author, as well as the children themselves. Then children arranged the cutouts, moved them around, talked about how they positioned themselves in relation to the identities and world deployed in the story. Davies (1993) explores the "radical possibility of giving children the capacity to disrupt the dominant storylines through which their gender is held in place" (p. 1). Specifically, she describes efforts to help elementary school students employ ideas of power, desire, discourse, and positioning, to examine how gender is constituted through various visual and written materials. Davies and Enciso suggest one way, then, to help students listen carefully to others' stories: We can give them access to critical concepts such as power and positioning, concepts that help students talk about and back to how stories focus and order readers' identities and worlds.

My move to critical talk about stories is, however, premature. A second responsibility in deliberation is exactly that we *not* move to criticism too quickly. Instead, we must *actively seek to understand* what others are saying. For Bernstein (1992), this requires effort and imagination, requires the attempt to "grasp the other's position in the strongest possible light" (p. 337). In a debate, we might pay particular attention to our doubts about an adversary's ideas, and then use these doubts to expose the other's position at its weakest points. But in deliberation—at least in the beginning, when we are trying to make sense of ideas different from our own—we must instead use our imaginative powers to represent others' ideas as forcefully as we can our own. Wayne Booth (1988) makes a similar point when he asserts that we must "surrender" to others' stories. He sees this move as indispensable to any later act of criticism:

> The essential first step, the step that provides data with which criticism of narrative deals, can only be that primary act of *assent* that occurs when we surrender to a story and follow it through to its conclusion. That act of assent will usually include assent to innumerable occasions for critical doubt offered by the author . . . But we discover the powers of any narrative only in an act of surrender. (p. 32)[8]

Booth's talk of surrender to the powers of stories evokes Dewey's description of the emotionally charged quality of deliberation, its "sensitiveness" and "vibrating response" to "every shade of imagined circumstance." It also points to the third responsibility our students take up in deliberation—that they be *open to learning, growth, changing their minds*.

Bernstein (1992) writes of "the courage to risk one's more cherished pre-judgments," but for me, even talk of courage and risks to cherished beliefs understates what is at stake (p. 51). Changing your mind means changing your habits, your dispositions to act, think, and feel in certain ways; it means changing your self. James Garrison (1997) gives us a better feel for this responsibility's repercussions:

> When we grow . . . we must become someone else. When our personal iden-tity changes, our relationships will change. Will those whose love sustains us—our parents, our friends, our children—continue to love us if we change? If we grow, not everyone in our web of relationships will respond to us as they did before. Why should they, since we are not the same? (p. 48)

Listening carefully, seeking actively to understand others' ideas, re-maining open to growth—these are difficult obligations I propose for stu-dents to honor during sharing time. We do not usually honor them as adults and teachers. But even when we do, even when our students do, trouble is our lot. When we proceed to deliberate in good faith, dangers follow (our inevitable failings speed their arrival).

One is what Bernstein (1992) calls the "false we"—when a sense of shared understanding is achieved more through projection or silencing others than through dialogue (p. 51). A second, related danger is to under-estimate how difficult it might actually be to understand another's world and traditions. Bernstein writes that we must be vigilant against "think-ing we can always easily translate what is alien into our own entrenched vocabularies." Instead, we may need first to learn another vocabulary—we may need to surrender to others' words for much longer than it takes to tell a story—before we can "recognize the ways in which rival traditions are and are not translatable" (p. 336).

A third danger is that we overestimate the efficacy of polite conversa-tion—that we assume that friendly talk assures everyone the chance to make themselves understood. It does not. As Bernstein puts it:

> Sometimes what is required to communicate—to establish a reciprocal "we"—is rupture and break—a *refusal* to accept the common ground laid down by the "other." . . . It is a self-deceptive illusion to think that the "other" can al-ways be heard in a friendly dialogue" (p. 52).

I remember well just such a rupture, a break, in a friendly dialogue I had just begun with my third grade students. I was launching a biography project in which students would write about important women in their lives. I told them that we would collect and publish their biographies in a book that we would then donate to the school's library. I told them that I had already talked to the librarian, and that she had agreed to assign their book an official call number and type up cards for the card catalog. I told them that this book was important, because when I had gone to the library and looked at the biography section, the shelves bore ten books about men to every one about women. I said that we all knew this wasn't right, since women were just as important as men. Their book would begin balancing things out.

John raised his hand and asserted politely that the reason there were more books about men in the library was probably because men were stronger and did more important things. Even as John spoke I recognized this as a "teachable moment"—as a moment to teach about gender and inequality, as well as teach third graders about how we conduct ourselves in classroom discussions on important topics. I don't wear jackets with patches on the arms; I don't smoke a pipe; I was standing and not sitting at the time. But before John had finished speaking, I was, at least in my imagination, settling back into a chair, crossing my legs, slowly blowing out smoke from a pipe. Maybe a dramatic pause, then: "Well, what do other people think about this?"

I never had the chance to blow my smoke. As John finished, Suzanne jumped out of her desk and asserted less politely that she would show John who's stronger at recess. Then she must have decided that she didn't really want to wait that long; she started toward John. With the scraping of chairs and gleeful chants of "Fight! Fight!" in the air, I suspended this particular deliberation and helped Suzanne back to her chair.[9]

We might interpret Suzanne's action as a failure to live up to the responsibilities of deliberation (and my failure to teach them). Perhaps she did not seek to put John's remarks in their best possible light. But we can also interpret her move as a necessary refusal to occupy John's all-too-common ground. Suzanne's promise to demonstrate her body's power upon John's body disrupted the dialogue. But would a polite questioning of John's story about stronger men commanding more space in the biography section have communicated as much? Would it have suggested as forcefully to John and others Suzanne's "vibrating response" to this line of action?

The fourth and final danger facilitates each of the previous three—that we confuse what it is we want, what we desire in and from deliberation. The danger can be made plain by considering what "shared in common" means.

Bernstein (1992) is clear: "There can be no dialogue, no communication unless beliefs, values, commitments, and even emotions and passions are shared in common" (p. 51). So is Dewey (1916/1966):

> There is more than a verbal tie between the words common, community, and communication. Men live in a community in virtue of the things which they have in common; and communication is the way in which they come to possess things in common. What they must have in common in order to form a community or society are aims, beliefs, aspirations, knowledge—a common understanding. (p. 4)

I confess that such lines from Bernstein and Dewey give me the willies. I worry that they are saying that the goal of deliberation is, in the end, for everyone to become the same, to think, feel, act the same. But this is a serious mistake. "Shared in common" and "possess things in common"—these do not point to how people might be alike, to shared or common characteristics. John and Suzanne, for example, both had rather quick tempers—they "possessed" these "in common." This is not what Bernstein and Dewey are talking about.

Think of a belief or value or passion or aspiration as a material thing set on a table (if it helps, think of a bible or a meal). Then think of this thing as *shared* by three people who are sitting around the table. Two people have warm feelings for it; one doesn't. The first loves the thing so much that a large part of his identity is wrapped up with working on it. The second hates the thing; she spends much of her time and energy avoiding or criticizing it. The last loves the other two people and is just happy to share something with them. The thing, however—the meal, bible, the belief, value, passion, aspiration—is there between them. It is shared in common.

Deliberation does not aim at making people think and feel and act the same. We endanger deliberation when we confuse a desire for sharing with a desire for sameness. Differences as well as similarities, agreements as well as disagreements, can be set on the table. As for the bearing of students' stories and responses during sharing time—they don't all need to aim in the same direction to be part of a common activity and understanding:

> To pull at a rope at which others happen to be pulling is not a shared or conjoint activity, unless the pulling is done *with knowledge* that others are pulling and *for the sake of either helping or hindering* what they are doing. . . . [If] each views the consequences of his own acts as having a bearing upon what others are doing and takes into account the consequences of their behavior upon himself, then there is a common mind; a common intent of behavior. There is an *understanding* set up between *different* contributors; and this common understanding controls the action of each. (Dewey, 1916/1966, p. 30; emphasis added)

Teachers are responsible for encouraging this plural and common understanding in the writing workshop. When we ask students to participate responsibly in deliberation, we ask something arduous. Even more is demanded of workshop teachers. Not only do they participate in deliberation themselves with students; they also organize it, make sure it happens in the first place. Obviously, part of making it happen is helping students write stories—otherwise there is nothing to talk about. Here, however, I focus on responsibilities teachers take up for sharing time.

As organizers and conductors of deliberation, teachers teach its responsibilities. They teach critical concepts and techniques that help students hear consequences, in others' rehearsals of experience, for their own. They make judgments of when to intervene in and interrupt students' ongoing deliberations—to enforce polite conversation, to support ruptures of politeness for the sake of communication.

As participants and players in deliberation—and in addition to listening carefully, seeking to understand, and remaining open to growth—teachers take on at least two more responsibilities. First, they stand with the underdog; they take sides. Fairness demands it. Friendship groups—in their stories and responses to stories—draw on cultural resources already marked, already validated and denigrated, by dominant groups in communities and societies outside the workshop. Friendship groups that align themselves with dominant story lines are well-positioned to dominate deliberation. They benefit from repeated access to occasions and sites in which authorized meanings and values are practiced, extended, and defended. They will often sound more reasonable, persuasive—sometimes because the telling example comes quickly and well-formed (because a lot of money and time has been spent elsewhere developing and telling it); sometimes just because their stories and responses sound familiar.

The macropolitics of social and cultural struggle hook up, here, with the micropolitics of face-to-face interaction among members of different friendship groups. Davies (1993), for example, in her analysis of a deliberation among fifth and sixth grade students about a recent news story, found that boys undermined the claims and stories of girls by citing the exclusion of women from certain professional sports. The news story concerned a woman who had sailed around the world by herself, and Davies notes that the conversation began with talk about *adult women* and whether or not they could be heroic. Soon, however, the "boy's attack is on *girls*" and it is accomplished, in part, by boys' assertions that women cannot play male sports such as football (p. 71). Now, girls sitting directly in front of these boys played these sports. But by invoking a division and hierarchy between men and women in the adult world, boys were able, in this instance, to separate themselves off from girls and dominate the conversation. Thus:

> Although the girls can and do play the boys' sports, the fact that women are
> excluded from them in the adult games is not just a problem for the future
> but something that impacts on their idea of who they are now. The rules of
> adult sport will exclude them. Their sameness now [with boys] is eroded and
> undermined by that social fact. *The boys can use that knowledge of social struc-*
> *ture to gain ascendancy over the girls and to dismiss the everyday evidence of their*
> *competence.* (p. 72)

Unless we are willing to stand by and sanction the reproduction of larger patterns of relation and domination within deliberation, teachers need, at times, to lend their knowledge and power to certain students—need to stand with them. Think of it as trying, as best they can, to join particular friendship groups for a while. Or, in Collins's (1991) terms, cited above, the teacher attempts to participate in principled coalitions with individuals and friendship groups for the purpose of institutional transformation (in this case, the transformation of everyday talk during sharing time).

This won't be easy. Students might reject the proposed coalition. Whom to stand with and when may be difficult to determine, since students' distinctions of who is us and them and in and out will change, sometimes from moment to moment. In addition, even as other responsibilities such as listening carefully and surrendering to others' stories demand suspending judgment, this responsibility demands that the teacher make critical (if shifting) distinctions between those students and ideas she affirms and those she opposes.

Still, the fact that we live in a classist, white supremacist, patriarchal, and heterosexist society gives us some beginning clues as to which students may find themselves positioned as undesirable in deliberation. If we truly want all voices to sound during sharing time, teachers will have to persuade these students that their voices are actually desired, no matter the disruption to dominant story lines, the rupture of polite talk. This is especially important since not just these students, but most students, learn that silence and obedience are what is expected and rewarded. bell hooks (1994) links the usual decorum of classroom life—with its avoidance of conflict and dissent—to the dominance of bourgeois values in schools. Bourgeois values condemn "loudness, anger, emotional outbursts, and even something as seemingly innocent as unrestrained laughter" as "unacceptable, vulgar disruptions of classroom social order," as traits "associated with being a member of the lower classes" (p. 178). Students learn that—as my Grandma Lensmire would have said it—they *mustn't* do these things.

What is acceptable and desirable *must be expanded* if students' beliefs, values, passions, and aspirations are ever going to get shared, become common, during sharing time.

This points to the final teacher responsibility for sharing time—that the teacher bring story lines to deliberation that are not necessarily represented in students' stories, so as to expand, again, what is available as direction for living. This responsibility is sometimes lived out during sharing time, but its demands spread to all the work the teacher pursues with her students, all the work that might be remembered, retold, appropriated for sharing time. Sometimes, the teacher multiplies students' story worlds by sharing stories from his own life; more often, by giving students access to stories told and written by others outside the workshop, from the near and far past.

I have backed us into the whirling, churning (do I smell something burning?) questions of canon and curriculum, questions of what is worthy and important for our students to learn in schools. I will pull us away quickly. But before I do, I note that the teacher responsibilities I have outlined for deliberation—in terms of helping students learn to *write*—might just as easily be interpreted as responsibilities teachers take up to help students learn to *read and criticize texts*. To experience the meanings and values of stories, to surrender to their direction, is to read them. To then deliberate their direction—to attend to "human, ethical, and political reactions" in order to appraise meanings and values and how these are produced—is to criticize them (Scholes, 1985, p. 23). Thus, deliberation is aimed, in part, at criticism, at helping students pursue critical explorations and evaluations of other students' stories.

I say "in part" because, important as criticism is, it is not all that we want. Criticism takes up already existing meanings and values in stories, already existing alternatives. It does not involve the creation of new alternatives. In a world marked both by continuous change and by the reproduction of oppressive structures, we want—we want and need—new stories. We want and need stories that reconstruct the old worlds deployed in old stories. We want and need, as Garrison (1997) so forcefully argues, *poetry* and *prophecy*: *that which imagines "what is absent yet present in our need"* and *that which names the "values needed in needful times"* (p. xvi).[10]

I don't mean to deny the creativity and imagination demanded by criticism. I don't mean to imply some sort of strong distinction between criticism and creation. In his final riff on Matthew Arnold's line that "poetry is criticism of life," Dewey (1934/1989) emphasizes that the "most penetrating criticism" is, in the end, the imaginative vision of an artist that helps us see unrealized possibilities: "It is by a sense of possibilities opening before us that we become aware of constrictions that hem us in and of burdens that oppress" (p. 349). Similarly, Paulo Freire (1985) intones (with religious overtones) that "there is no annunciation without denunciation, just as every denunciation generates annunciation" (p. 58). Toni Morrison (1992) notes that reading and writing, criticism and creation, harmonize for the writer in pursuit of her art:

> Both exercises require being alert and ready for unaccountable beauty, for the intricateness or simple elegance of the writer's imagination, for the world that imagination evokes. Both require being mindful of the places where imagination sabotages itself, locks its own gates, pollutes its vision. (p. xi)

To say all that—even when done so wonderfully well by Dewey and Freire and Morrison—is not to say that criticism and creation cannot be distinguished, at certain moments and for certain purposes, to good effect. I distinguish them here for two reasons. First, by attending to each in turn, I can provide a richer account of what it takes to support learning to write in classrooms. In my discussion of sharing time, I have concentrated on *criticism*, on students listening to and reading and deliberating other students' stories. In deliberation, students come to recognize some of the possibilities embodied in stories inherited from and created with their pasts and close friends. Students also come to recognize some of the limits of these stories, and that there are others. In what follows, I concentrate on *creation*, on the conditions that might support the writing of transgressive stories.

My second reason for distinguishing between criticism and creation is to make sure we understand into what sort of trouble we are headed. Creation, like carnival profanation, is ambivalent, both destructive and regenerating. Its pursuit may very well be more dangerous and violent than the pursuit of criticism. I say more about this later. For now, I cite Jacques Derrida's summons that we take up criticism tirelessly, perpetually. We may never succeed in removing violence from our world, but we can, as Derrida writes,

> Try to recognize and analyze [it] as best we can in its various forms: obvious or disguised, institutional or individual, literal or metaphoric, candid or hypocritical, in good or guilty conscience. And if, as I believe, violence remains in fact (almost) ineradicable, its analysis and the most refined, ingenious account of its conditions will be the least violent gestures, perhaps even non-violent, and in any case those which contribute most to transforming the legal-ethical-political rules. (cited in Bernstein, 1992, p. 217)

I share with Derrida the belief that violence is pretty much ineradicable, and I have tried as best I can in this book and in *When Children Write* to pay attention to various forms of violence in the writing workshop. Furthermore, I agree that sophisticated analyses of violence like the ones Derrida produces are (perhaps) non-violent, (but in any event) important contributions to rewriting society's directions.

I get lost, however, at Derrida's "most" in "contribute *most* to transforming the legal-ethical-political rules." Compared to what? Unless his category of "refined, ingenious accounts" has space and time for the prophet's *annunciation*, for the poet's *imaginative vision*, I think that Derrida has it wrong.[11] Criticism may very well be less violent than creation. But that doesn't mean that it contributes more to transformation (it may mean it contributes less).

Criticism is not *self* sufficient. It needs stories to rehearse on. And I doubt that we can make our *selves* up out of doubt.[12] We need stories. And if we want to make ourselves and our worlds up differently, then we need different stories.

Story Time

> I had become paralysed . . . I was pondering all of the elements of story telling that may unwittingly reconstitute the gender order that any feminist story is attempting to undo, worrying about how to be aware enough to remove them all, and beginning to realise that that is actually impossible . . . Any story has to incorporate what we know already if it is to be comprehensible, if it is to be pleasurable enough to capture the reader's imagination. It must do both of these if it is to move us on to a new possibility different from the ones we know already. (Davies, 1993, p. 190)

Even when a writer sets out to create a transgressive story, her story will unavoidably be a mix of old and new. As Davies reminds us, it is impossible to undo, all at once, all the forms, beliefs, meanings, and values upon which the writer must draw in order to communicate. Some things will have to be left intact, closed, assumed, already answered, in order for other things to be broken, opened up, un-assumed, questioned, and re-answered (or left unresolved).[13]

There are many ways—involving any to many of the "elements of story

"We come as clouds, the . . ." the class recited together, practising for the evening's performance.

"WE COME AS CLOUD," yelled Manuel, walking into the classroom.
Sinead rolled her eyes.

telling"—for a story to be transgressive. And the reader, of course, can be more or less attentive to what is different. The reader can rehearse the story in ways that emphasize new questions and new answers, or old ones; the reader can refuse to rehearse at all. If the reader is generous and shares her deliberation with the writer, the writer can learn about his story—what was comprehensible, what captured the imagination, what was old and new.

Thus, creation—where creation is distinguished from criticism and from old stories—ultimately depends on both. A generous supply of old stories

"Guess what? We're going to read *The Christmas Carol*," said Joanie as she came over to Cheryl and Robert.

and a generous criticism are necessary conditions for the flourishing of creation.

"Yes!" yelled Robert.

"Yes!" yelled Manuel, jumping up and down.

"I already knew that," said Cheryl.

In what follows, I return one last time to the workshop as learning environment and community of writers, in order to review and extend my account of how it supports creation. I emphasize a particular sort of creation and transgression: the production of student-authored stories that direct students to cross boundary lines that divide them from other people, stories that imagine others as possible sources of learning, meaning, value, friendship, and love.

How do writing workshops—the workshops I have affirmed, criticized, and reconstructed across the pages of this book—support the writing of creative, transgressive stories? I recount five ways.

The first is simply the invitation to students to write stories. Besides making material available for deliberation and others' learning, this invitation makes possible the expression of unique, unexpected visions. For the question isn't

Just then, Mrs. Smith came on the speaker. "Boys and girls, may I have your attention."

whether students will transgress in their writing—we should expect

"No you can't," thought Sinead.

the unexpected from children and young adults—but whether or not these transgressions will be noticed, recognized when they happen, surrendered to long enough for their possibilities to be explored by students and teachers.

The second creation-supporting feature of workshops is their acceptance of student-chosen friendship groups. Friendship groups can close off contact with others and support the writing of stories that do the same. But the acceptance of friendship groups that reproduce and contribute to divisions among students along race, social class, and gender lines is also the acceptance of friendship groups that transgress these lines. When students see and hear what others are and say (and are curious and like it) and desire new classmates with whom to conference and collaborate, the work-shop's space and time for student-chosen groups is transgressive.

"Students in the gym, may I have your attention."

"I'm not in the gym, so I don't HAVE to pay attention," thought Sinead again.

The third way that workshops support transgression is in their dis-order, their carnival quality, their mess and mix of stories and bodies. School tasks are broken and remade; conventional student and teacher roles abandoned, new ones tried on, played. Workshops make available expe-riences with others and the world that are unavailable in traditional class-rooms. They create possibilities for a transgressive sort of living that then might be reported, pushed further in imagination, written down.

I worry that as we up the ante of our goals for workshops (as I have, as we must), we might lose sight of how important this aspect of work-shops is. Sometimes, seriousness of purpose leads to somberness, tighten-ing up, a fearfulness of failing in an important endeavor. As we become more "serious," we risk undermining the sort of joyful, playful relation to the world and each other that would actually allow us to look fearlessly at the world and tell the truth about it, as best we can. In other words, in order to criticize and rewrite the world and stories in the workshop, we and students will need to play (with ideas, with each other) in order to experience and imagine something better—a something better that throws the present's shortcomings into bold relief. Seriousness can undermine truthfulness, and criticism may require child's play. I have always liked Madeleine Grumet's (1988) call for us to look to our "daughters' lies," their fantasies of how things could be, for help in redeeming our own and our children's lives:

> In showing us the world as they would have it, they reveal the world that we fled because we were not brave enough to pitch our tents and raise our flags there. Their lies

"Remember to have your best manners on tonight and great voices. We want our parents to be impressed, don't we? Of course we do."

"Not me," thought Sinead to herself.

"Good afternoon."

RRRRRRRRRRRIIIIIIIIIIIINNNNNNNNNNNGGGGGGGGGG. The bell rang.

"Try to wear something nice tonight," said Mrs. Cliffrie.

> can become our knowledge. (p. 162)

I have not addressed the fourth creation-supporting feature of work-shops in this book, and I do little more than mention it here. Lucy Calkins

(1991) has called for the addition of "genre studies" to workshop approaches, in which students and teachers put aside student-chosen writing projects from time to time and focus their attention on learning about a particular genre of text. This is good, as far as it goes—what Calkins proposes can help students understand how different types of text work, are put together. We can imagine such work leading to playful variations and reconstructions of the genres studied. Once again, however, workshop advocates avoid critical appraisals of texts, avoid criticism of content, or work that explores how different genres are valued and devalued by more and less powerful groups in various situations. Luckily, directions for a more meaning-and-value-attending, politicized, and transgressive version of genre studies can be found.[14]

Clifford, Friesen, and Jardine (1995), for example, tell how they explored native stories with Sinead, Manuel, and their classmates—they all read picture books, listened to storytellers, drew pictures, examined the art of native illustrators and artists. Nothing so radical, I suppose (the study of native people is even part of the prescribed curriculum in Alberta, Canada, where the authors work). But what *particular* stories you study in your genre studies makes a difference, doesn't it? They studied Coyote stories.

"Ayeeeya aeeeeya," sang the choir, beginning a native song.

Old Man Coyote is one of the First People who created the world and human life and culture. One of Coyote's gifts to us is fire, which he stole from the "upriver end of the world."[15] But Coyote, as William Bright (1993) emphasizes, is no "Promethean hero":

> He is an insatiable glutton, a gross lecher, an inveterate thief, liar, and outlaw, a prankster whose schemes regularly backfire. In short, Coyote is the archetypal Trickster known from literatures all over the world—Renard the Fox of medieval French legend, and Anansi the Spider of West African and modern Afro-Caribbean tradition. (p. 3)

This is who Clifford, Friesen, and Jardine (1995) invited into a *primary school classroom.* (Goodness gracious.)

This is why:

> Calling to us from the boundaries of our own world, Coyote howls holes in the taken-for-granted [and] invites us "in" through such openings, such opportunities for understanding . . . He teaches. And he teaches by teaching us the limits of the world. And he teaches such limits through their violation. (pp. 8, 9)

They report that almost all of the children in the class wrote Coyote stories. The children weren't asked or required to write stories about Coyote—they just did. This genre study incorporated the transgressive "feral agency of Coyote herself"

Coyote, coming in the door, heard a wonderful singing. After his hard day with Grandfather Rock, he sure did feel like singing—especially when they got to the part with the "Harpooooooooooooooooooooooooooon him?" That tricky Coyote, he started singing along with the choir. OOOOOOOOOOOOOOOOOOOOOO. OOOOOO. OOOOOOOO OOOOOOOOOOOOOOOOOO. OOOOOOOO.

into the imaginations and stories of children (p. 9).

For me, the most developed and generative account of genre studies—of what genre studies *could be* in writing workshops—is Carol Lee's (1993) book on signifying and the teaching of literary interpretation. Lee traces the processes and results of a project that involved teachers and black students from six classrooms in two urban high schools. The project sought to bring students' and community-based knowledge to bear in classroom instruction. More specifically, Lee's project explored how signifying—a form of social discourse—might be drawn upon to teach students to read and make sense of difficult, complex fiction.

Lee explains that, within the African American community, to *signify* means to "speak with innuendo and double meanings, to play rhetorically upon the meaning and sounds of words, and to be quick and often witty in one's response" (p. 11). In other words,

"What fun," thought Coyote to himself.

signifying demands producing and responding to the sort of metaphoric and ironic language that is often encountered in literature (and that often baffles or alienates novice readers). Lee claims, then, that many African American adolescents bring to literature classes a "powerful intellectual tool which goes unnoticed, devalued, and untapped": their signifying capacities (p. 13). In her research and writing, Lee tests—and ultimately redeems—this claim. She demonstrates that the signifying powers of black youth can indeed be mobilized to good effect in the interpretation of rich and complex literary texts.

But not very many parents in the audience thought that listening to OOOOOOOOOOOOOOOOOOOOOOOOO was the most pleasant way to spend the Christmas concert.

"Who's making that racket?" someone whispered to Zoe's dad.

"I don't know," said Don under his breath, "but it certainly isn't Zoe or Jeremy."

Lee's project was transgressive—at a minimum, doubly. It reached across the usual white, bourgeois values of schooling to embrace black youth and their language. It also embraced African American fiction as worthy of study in schools. Black texts trespassed the white canon in Lee's project, and this gave students the chance to feel at home even as their worlds were expanded, questioned, remade in the imaginative visions of black authors. Lee was not concerned with investigating how such literary study might influence the stories students write. But I can't help feeling that transgression breeds transgression, and that the students in her project were ready to write creative stories, transgressive stories that howled holes in the taken-for-granteds and limits that we assume and impose, that they endure.

If they weren't ready—that is, if Lee's project is to be extended in some way to help students produce transgressive stories—then what about this: that teachers focus explicit attention and discussion on moments of transgression in literature and how they are produced, and then tell students to go try that in their writing. In his work on gender and genre, John Willinsky (1995) argues that such moves will help students experiment with *"writing against,* rather than the far more intimidating *writing with,* the masters, finding a place within the folds of their great cloaks to tug at their ears, turn their collars around" (p. 253). For what it's worth—when I revisit Bakhtin's book on Rabelais and carnival, it often seems less a literary or philosophical study and more a teacher's or writer's guide filled with lessons on how you too can transgress in speech and writing. "Today, we will practice degrading superiors. One strategy is to compare some aspect of their face to an animal or to another part of the human body (preferably from the lower bodily stratum). For example, the chancellor has a small nose that looks like . . ." (see Bakhtin, 1984b, p. 316).

Robert's mum turned to look. "Oh no, Don. I can't believe it. That's not a child at all. It's a big dog or something."

The fifth and final way that (reconstructed) workshops support transgression is in their deliberation about stories. Deliberation teaches students what their stories mean and gives them the chance to write similar or different stories next time, with a better sense of how their writing influences others. Dewey (1916/1966) reminds us that

> Activity begins in an impulsive form; that is, it is blind. It does not know what it is about; that is to say, what are its interactions with other activities. An activity which brings education or instruction with it makes one aware of some of the connections which had been imperceptible. (p. 77)

As writers, we and students are blind to many of the meanings and consequences of our texts. Deliberation about stories helps students learn what their writing is about, helps them see and feel how it interacts with the stories and lives of others, helps them begin to understand the powers and responsibilities of writing. Without deliberation, without access to others' responses, students are cut off from instruction that would help them take greater control over and responsibility for their literate activity.

However, even in workshops characterized by deliberation, the activity *begins* in impulsive form, *is blind*. And this is dangerous. Teachers take risks (even risk their jobs) when they encourage creation—for creation demands openness to the unpredictable, the unknown, in schools, and the one thing usually required of teachers is that they stay in control, keep order.

"Oh don't be ridiculous, Pam. There can't be a dog in here. It must be someone's child." And he turned around to see whether it was anybody he knew.

Even when teachers have external support for their work inside workshops, creation and transgression are dangerous. If writing begins blind, then students' stories *will* sometimes hurt and do violence to others, whether the writers intend it or not. Students and teachers can try to minimize the hurt, can take steps to decrease the likelihood of violence.[16] But if workshops are open to the creative activity of students, then they are open. And that means monsters[17] and outlaws[18] will walk in the door.

"Oh NO! It's a coyote. A coyote. COYOTE AT THE CHRISTMAS CONCERT!" And he fainted dead away.

Pandora's Pedagogy—that's the name Deborah Britzman (1991) gives to the sort of teaching and living I have proposed. Britzman assures us that such a pedagogy will unleash *unpopular things* in the classroom and let them roam about. We will witness powerful, even creative, renderings of truly ugly ideas—renderings that reassert dominant meanings and values, that "subvert the fragile coalition that depends upon concern for others" (p. 64). We will witness imagined worlds that undermine our arguments and hopes for more democracy.

So why do this? Why would we ask teachers and students to risk this danger and violence?

Because

Suddenly, from the other side of the gym, a sound started to build.

such a pedagogy will *unleash* unpopular things in the classroom

It was Coyote number two, Manuel the Magnificent.

and let them roam about.

He wanted to sing,

Monsters disrupt our complacency, our easy common sense of what is normal, right.

and he did.

Outlaws are outside the law, sometimes, not because they are bad, but because they are good.

And guess what?

Sinead, a little kid, understood this, did this. With her teachers' and Coyote's help, she imagined a classroom and school (and concert) that had space and time for Manuel and his voice. She denounced specialist and reasoned pronouncements of who Manuel was, and offered a generous and crazy (like a fox) alternative for his present and future. Sinead made Manuel into a big howling dog. That should be bad. But it's good. Sinead made Manuel into Old Man Coyote Number Two—Sinead imagined Manuel as one who teaches by transgression, as one who might teach her if she listened carefully. I think we should listen carefully to these children.

Why should we do this? Because we will witness powerful, creative visions that teach us about unrealized possibilities and unregarded others. Because

Everyone else started singing and even Sinead was happy and they had the best Christmas Concert ever—at least for that year.

we will rehearse truly beautiful stories that strengthen our hopes for democracy. And let us live it.

NOTES

1. As discussed in chapter 3, workshop advocates effect this wishing by focusing on individual writers and by assuming a happy, inclusive classroom. When friendship groups and conflict among children are recognized by writing educators and researchers, we tend to get stories with happy endings—that is, reports of instances when divisions and conflict are worked through to a more inclusive social setting or literary vision (see, for example, Dyson, 1993; 1997). However, it is simply not inevitable that things will work out well.

2. This claim is revised later in the chapter. Given the sort of society in which we live, given the divisions and hierarchies within which our children are learning to be human, we can be sure that ugly things will be said and done within the workshop. Thus, not only does increased student control offer no guarantees that students will interact and communicate in desirable ways; it guarantees that, at least some of the time, they will not.

3. Dewey (1934/1989) himself cautions that words like "standard" and "measure" suggest the determination of *quantity* and the use of an "external and public thing, defined by law to be the same for all transactions, that can be physically applied" (for example, a yardstick), rather than the *qualitative* judgment of value (p. 310, 311).

4. I use "embryonic" here because Dewey (1899/1980) uses it in *The School and Society* when he calls on schools to be embryonic democratic communities. That is, I want to associate Dewey with Collins's (1991) project. I understand that Collins's project and black women's struggle may seem to be doubly diminished by my moves here, by associating them with (1) children, and (2) an old white academic. Furthermore, my moves could be interpreted as making Collins's ideas

more palatable for readers from dominant groups, could be interpreted as doing exactly what Collins says often happens: "Oppressed groups are frequently placed in the situation of being listened to only if we frame our ideas in the language that is familiar to and comfortable for a dominant group" (p. xiii). Readers will have to judge for themselves. All I can say is that my intent runs pretty much exactly in the opposite direction: I hope to lend some dignity and significance to the struggles of children by associating them with the struggles of black women; I hope to lend some credibility to an often glibly interpreted educational philosopher by associating him with a contemporary theorist; and I hope to create, with the use of Collins and Dewey, the sort of discomfort that comes with engaging different and powerful ideas.

5. This is Dewey's (1916/1966) analysis of direction; see pp. 23–36. I take responsibility for the duck joke. "That's going to leave a mark" is a recurring line from the movie *Tommy Boy*, starring the late Chris Farley.

6. Johnson (1993) writes: "Narrative explorations . . . are, in fact, what moral reasoning is all about" (cited in Garrison, 1997, p. 147).

7. I follow Caspary (1995) here. He writes that even as Dewey "presents his account of deliberation in terms of the private thoughts of a single individual," Dewey also emphasizes that "the various 'voices' within this person's mind amount to the transposition of a public conversation" (p. 24).

8. I am not saying that we have to surrender over and over again to stories we know will hurt us or not teach us. But, as Booth (1988) explores wonderfully well, there is a problem here—we can't learn if a story will benefit us until after we give ourselves over to it.

9. John and Suzanne faced off on another occasion—they actually got their hands on each other that time. See Lensmire (1994), chapter 4.

10. See Garrison (1997), especially chapter 5, for a powerful and beautiful rendering of what he calls Dewey's "critical-creative theory of intelligent deliberation and the education of eros" (p. 127).

11.   a

Let's be serious.

I am in no position (where? me?) even to pretend to make a statement about Derrida.

b

Since I had read and understood enough of Derrida in other places to know that he is very hard to understand, I wanted to make sure—even though I trust Bernstein more than most writers—that he had cited Derrida responsibly. So I went to the Washington University Olin Library and found out that it didn't have the English version of Derrida's *Limited Inc*, which Bernstein had cited. It did have a copy of what I assumed was the original French version, but when I went to the shelves, that wasn't there. I picked up a Derrida reader (I mean a collection of his writings, not someone who reads Derrida—not that there is anything wrong with that), hoping that Derrida's text would be inside. It wasn't. I ignored the main text of the reader and focused on the footnotes, and found that *Limited Inc* was originally published in something called *Glyph 2*, and, praise the gods (I did this silently, with eyes and hands pointed upward, but in diverse directions), the library had that.

So I had my copy of Derrida, and in English so I didn't have to impose on friends to read it in French for me. (It turns out that Derrida wrote it in French, but knew it was going to be translated right away into English by Samuel Weber—Derrida mentions this right there in the body of the text. In fact, if Derrida can be believed, Weber started translating his text even before Derrida had written it. That must have been hard.) I took his (whose?) text home and started reading, but it was long, almost 100 pages, and I couldn't find the lines Bernstein had quoted anyway. To tell the truth, I got sort of nervous as I read Derrida's text, since it is (was?) a reply to some other people Derrida refers to collectively as "Sarl" (Derrida has his reasons), and Derrida was talking (oops, I should say writing) precisely (quite precisely) about *citation* and everything, and about how Sarl had screwed it up, both in theory and practice. I eventually got tired. Which is just as well, since I will have to conclude this section rather abruptly because Derrida appropriates *d* through *z* to organize his text, which means I've only got

©

I accept Staten's (1984) characterization of Derrida's writing as "neither poetry nor (quite) philosophy" (p. xiv); I'll call it very creative criticism. I am still not sure what that "contribute *most* to transforming the legal-ethical-political rules" (my emphasis, I think) meant. But I am comfortable with my criticism of Derrida. First, if you look closely, it's not much of one anyway. If his category of "refined, ingenious accounts" *does* have room for creation, then there's nothing for me to confront him about—we can just be friends (he will never read this anyway). I know he could show me hundreds of places where he makes room for and defends and even exalts creation (though he certainly wouldn't like that word much). Look at this:

> Once iterability has established the possibility of parasitism, of a certain fictionality altering at once—*Sec* too [*aussi sec*]—the system of (il- or perlocutionary) intentions and the systems of ("vertical") rules or of ("horizontal") conventions, inasmuch as they are included within the scope of iterability; once this parasitism or fictionality can always add *another* parasitic or fictional structure to *whatever* preceded it—what I elsewhere designate as a "supplementary code" ["*supplement de code*"]—everything becomes possible against the language-police; for example, "literatures" or "revolutions" that as yet have no model. Everything is possible except for an exhaustive typology that would claim to limit the powers of graft or of fiction by and within an analytical logic of distinction, opposition, and classification in genus and species. (Derrida, 1977, p. 243; author's and translator's emphases, except for *whatever*, which is mine)

Second, I am comfortable because I trust that Bernstein (1992) has a good position, and I think that he wishes Derrida would (just every now and then, and of course in a tentative, fallibilistic sort of way) suggest some direction(s), make clearer what he thinks might be desirable: "We want some understanding of what kinds of institutions and practices should be developed for 'a democracy to come.' Or even more minimally, we want some orientation about what changes 'here and now' are needed in our present institutional structures" (Bernstein, 1992, p. 223). Bernstein is a generous critic, and he interprets this problem with Derrida's work as "not only Derrida's, but *our* collective problematic" (p. 191). So I conclude with another (maybe violent) appropriation and citation of Bernstein's text—a text that points (I think, I hope) to our need for new stories, new hypotheses for new worlds:

> [Derrida] presumably points us toward the promised land of a *postmetaphysical* ethics and politics without adumbrating its geography. Or perhaps, we might say "the promised land" that we may "dream" about is obscured by a hazy and foggy horizon. (p. 191)

12. Or maybe we can—but for me, the possible selves we might build out of *only* doubt seem undesirable. I do not have good ways of thinking about this yet. My hunch is that part of the problem is the sort of freedom that is imaginable for such selves—it would be only a skeptical freedom, which, as Bernstein asserts (1992), is "radically unstable" and "always in danger of becoming merely abstract" (p. 162). Hegel argued that skeptical freedom

> Ends up with the bare abstraction of nothingness or emptiness and cannot get any further from there, but must wait to see whether something new comes along and what it is, in order to throw it too into the empty abyss. (cited in Bernstein, 1992, p. 162)

I guess I would rather that we and children not always wait for someone else to come up with something new, even if what we produce eventually gets tossed.

13. Booth's (1988) discussion, pp. 60–70, is especially helpful on this point.

14. Genre-based approaches to the teaching of writing, developed primarily by Australian researchers and educators and, in part, in critical response to workshop approaches, are another resource. See Kamler (1994), Lee (1993), Richardson (1991), and Threadgold (1988) for discussions and criticisms of these approaches.

15. See Bright (1993), pp. 84–86.

16. For example, from conversations with a number of different teachers, it seems that the hurtful use of other students' names in stories (making classmates into characters) is a recurrent problem, and often leads to workshop rules prohibiting or regulating such practices. I discuss my own experiences with this in chapter 6 of Lensmire (1994).

17. For a discussion of "monstrous examples" and their importance to our efforts to democratize classrooms, see Field and Jardine (1994).

18. For discussions of the significance of outlaws and "outlaw emotions," see Garrison (1997) and Jaggar (1989).

Conclusion

I don't feel like reviewing prominent themes or promising future work, so I will look backward and forward in a different way. I will tell you a story. This story is about the literary and legal theorist Stanley Fish, the history of Western thought, my mom, John Dewey, my dad, Mikhail Bakhtin, a Catholic priest, sex, and me. It is a fun story. Much more fun than Fish's (1995) story about Western thought across the ages, but that's where I start.

The Fish story is that Western thought has been one long quarrel between two kinds of man. The one man is *homo seriosus*, SERIOUS MAN, who thinks that he has grabbed hold of the real world (as it really, really is) with his power of reason. (If you can remember as far back as chapter 2, then we could also call this one MONOLOGIC MAN, which sounds more like the superhero SERIOUS MAN usually imagines himself to be.) The other man is *homo rhetoricus*, RHETORICAL MAN, who pretty much thinks that the best we can do is talk the world over and make it up, as best we can, as we go along. If you paid attention at all as you read my book (or even just as you read this conclusion so far), then you know that, when push comes to shove, I stand with RHETORICAL MAN. So did Mikhail Bakhtin and John Dewey.

My feminist, pro-feminist, and psychoanalytically inclined readers will not be surprised to learn that it was actually a WOMAN—MY MOTHER—who introduced me to this quarrel and started me on the path to rhetoric. Actually, my mom and the Catholic Church.

Whatever else my grade school education at St. Mary School did, it confronted me directly, explicitly, early on, with basic existential questions: What is life? How should we live it? What does it mean? Even as I have fallen away from the church, I have not fallen away from the idea that I have to take these questions seriously, and that my life will be a more or less worthy answer to these questions.

Of course, St. Mary School provided me with the right answers to these questions.

My mom, Lynn Lensmire, was and is a sincere Catholic. She also was the catcher for her neighborhood baseball team (the rest were boys) when she was growing up. She also was and is the daughter of the late machinist and vocal defender of labor, Walter Manicke, and the daughter of Gladys

120

Manicke, who has given years of service to the Salvation Army and one Christmas told me about childhood summers she spent with her father (my great-grandfather) in the woods as he tended his still. Her job was to watch for planes flying overhead that might carry federal agents bent on stopping the illegal production of alcohol and looking for smoke.

My mom wasn't from "The Hill" in Wausau, Wisconsin—a sign, then (maybe even now), of wealth and status. But she excelled at Wausau High School in English and mathematics and science. And in debate (my mom still likes to argue).

When I was in grade school, Mom told me that I had to take the questions put to me in religion class very seriously, and that I had to listen carefully to the answers provided. But she also said that, in the end, I would have to come up with my own answers, even if that meant disagreeing with the Catholic Church. I knew that my mom disagreed and argued with the local priest, Father Geissler, about birth control and how to educate young people. (Father Geissler scared me silly when I was little, so I am making him into the bad guy of my story.) When my mom absolved me from absolute obedience to the serious answers of the Catholic Church, she set me up to question the answers of other authorities I would encounter as I grew up. She also set me up to question my own answers, the answers I gave to and for myself.

This freedom and responsibility often felt terrifying—this was serious. And of course there were plenty of other serious people who, unlike my mom, were intent on making sure that I knew and embodied not my own answers, but the right answers. The biggest one when I was a little boy was Father Geissler. He was a tall, loud, shouting man with an angry mouth and a severe crew cut. He wore a black cassock. In God's army, Father Geissler was a Marine.

When I was in sixth grade, all the sixth, seventh, and eighth grade boys had to go to a special evening meeting at school with our fathers. As if this wasn't bad enough, Father Geissler was going to talk at us—and talk at us about SEX.

Or should I say SIN. I sat next to my dad in a steel folding chair in the cafeteria. Father Geissler was standing in front, by a chalkboard. He was especially loud and angry (apparently some of the older boys—who? where?—were crossing gender lines, and he didn't like it). At one point, Father Geissler said that if we ever got an ERECTION, that was a SIN. To help out those of us who might learn better when the shouting is supplemented by other modes of communication, he drew a picture on the chalkboard. (I confess that I was a late bloomer and that all of this—despite the priest's powerful pedagogy—was just a bit theoretical, a bit beyond me, at the time. I was slow to grasp the topic at hand.)

Father Geissler finally finished. As my father and I walked out into the freezing Wisconsin night, he told me that I should take what Father Geissler said with a grain of salt. And as we shivered in the car on the way home, he started laughing, and told me about a time he went swimming with his friends in the Eau Pleine River. Lots of people were there, and Dad and his friends were hollering and wrestling in the water.

His friends decided it was time to go, and ran out onto the beach and started drying off. When they saw that Dad hadn't joined them (he stayed, crouching, in the water), they started yelling and waving to him to hurry up, it was time to go. It seemed like all the people on the beach were looking at him, waiting for him to get out of the water. But he couldn't, because of a fairly obvious SIN in his swim trunks.

My dad was laughing and I was laughing. For a moment, I didn't have to worry so much about controlling my body and keeping it pure. And the sometimes lonely prospect of growing up and having to answer all those existentialist questions about life and its meaning and how to live—that didn't seem so lonely if I could go swimming with my friends and talk to people like my dad.

From Lynn Lensmire and John Dewey and many others, I have learned that there are important questions to be answered through our lives, that we need to listen carefully to the answers provided by diverse others, and that we are responsible for putting forward our own answers, which will in turn, hopefully, be listened to, affirmed, questioned, rejected, revised.

From John Lensmire and Mikhail Bakhtin and many others, I have learned that to sustain life, we need to laugh and be with and enjoy each other. We need to tell stories and have our stories answered by other stories and questions, need to rehearse different ways of being and acting in the world, in a rich celebration and deliberation of what is and what could be.

The End.

References

Aronowitz, S., & Giroux, H. (1991). *Postmodern education: Politics, culture, & social criticism*. Minneapolis: University of Minnesota Press.

Atwell, N. (1987). *In the middle: Writing, reading, and learning with adolescents*. Portsmouth, NH: Boynton/Cook.

Au, K. (1993). *Literacy instruction in multicultural settings*. Orlando, FL: Harcourt Brace Jovanovich.

Bakhtin, M. M. (1981). *The dialogic imagination*. Austin: University of Texas Press.

Bakhtin, M. M. (1984a). *Problems of Dostoevsky's poetics* (C. Emerson, Trans.). Minneapolis: University of Minnesota Press.

Bakhtin, M. M. (1984b). *Rabelais and his world* (H. Iswolsky, Trans.). Bloomington: Indiana University Press.

Bakhtin, M. M. (1986). *Speech genres and other late essays*. Austin: University of Texas Press.

Belenky, M. F., Clinchy, B. M., Goldberger, N. R., & Tarule, J. M. (1986). *Women's ways of knowing: The development of self, voice, and mind*. New York: Basic Books.

Berlin, J. (1988). Rhetoric and ideology in the writing class. *College English, 50*(5), 477–494.

Bernstein, R. (1992). *The new constellation: The ethical-political horizons of modernity/ postmodernity*. Cambridge, MA: MIT Press.

Booth, W. (1984). Introduction. In M. M. Bakhtin, *Problems of Dostoevsky's poetics* (pp. xiii–xxvii). (C. Emerson, Trans.). Minneapolis: University of Minnesota Press.

Booth, W. (1988). *The company we keep: An ethics of fiction*. Berkeley: University of California Press.

Bourdieu, P., & Passeron, J. C. (1977). *Reproduction in education, society, and culture*. London: Sage.

Bowles, S., & Gintis, H. (1976). *Schooling in capitalist America*. New York: Basic Books.

Bowles, S., & Gintis, H. (1987). *Democracy and capitalism*. New York: Basic Books.

Bright, W. (1993). *A coyote reader*. Berkeley: University of California Press.

Britzman, D. (1991). Decentering discourses in teacher education: Or, the unleashing of unpopular things. *Journal of Education, 173*(3), 60–80.

Bruner, J. (1990). *Acts of meaning*. Cambridge, MA: Harvard University Press.

Burke, K. (1989). *On symbols and society*. Chicago: University of Chicago Press.

Burke, P. (1978). *Popular culture in early modern Europe*. New York: New York University Press.

Calkins, L. M. (1986). *The art of teaching writing*. Portsmouth, NH: Heinemann.

Calkins, L. M. (1991). *Living between the lines*. Portsmouth, NH: Heinemann.

Caspary, W. (1991). Ethical deliberation as dramatic rehearsal: John Dewey's theory. *Educational Theory, 41*(2), 175–188.

Caspary, W. (1995). *John Dewey as a comprehensive transformational theorist.* Political Science Paper No. 278, Department of Political Science, Washington University in St. Louis.

Cazden, C. B. (1986). Classroom discourse. In M. C. Wittrock (Ed.), *Handbook of research on teaching* (3rd ed.; pp. 432–463). New York: Macmillan.

Cazden, C. B. (1994). Foreword. In T. Lensmire, *When children write: Critical revisions of the writing workshop* (pp. vii–viii). New York: Teachers College Press.

Clifford, P., Friesen, S., & Jardine, D. (1995). *"Whatever happens to him happens to us": Reading coyote reading the world.* Paper presented at annual meeting of National Reading Conference, New Orleans. Available online at www.ucalgary.ca/~jardine.

Cohen, D. (1988). Teaching practice: Plus ça change. . . . In P. Jackson (Ed.), *Contributing to educational change: Perspectives on research and practice* (pp. 27–84). Berkeley, CA: McCutchan.

Collins, P. H. (1991). *Black feminist thought: Knowledge, consciousness, and the politics of empowerment.* New York: Routledge.

Davies, B. (1993). *Shards of glass: Children reading and writing beyond gendered identities.* Cresskill, NJ: Hampton.

Delpit, L. (1995). *Other people's children.* New York: New Press.

Derrida, J. (1977). Limited Inc a b c. . . . In S. Weber & H. Sussman, *Glyph 2* (pp. 162–254). Baltimore: John Hopkins University Press.

Dewey, J. (1922). *Human nature and conduct.* New York: Henry Holt.

Dewey, J. (1938). *Experience and education.* New York: Collier.

Dewey, J. (1951). Creative democracy—The task before us. In M. Fisch (Ed.), *Classic American philosophers* (pp. 389–394). New York: Appleton-Century-Crofts. (Original work published 1939)

Dewey, J. (1966). *Democracy and education.* New York: Free Press. (Original work published 1916)

Dewey, J. (1980). *The school and society.* Carbondale: Southern Illinois University Press. (Original work published 1899)

Dewey, J. (1989). Art as experience. In J. Boydston (Ed.), *John Dewey: The later works* (Vol. 10). Carbondale: Southern Illinois University Press. (Original work published 1934)

Dressman, M. (1993). Lionizing lone wolves: The cultural Romantics of literacy workshops. *Curriculum Inquiry, 23*(3), 245–263.

Dyson, A. H. (1993). *The social worlds of children learning to write in an urban primary school.* New York: Teachers College Press.

Dyson, A. H. (1995). Writing children: Reinventing the development of childhood literacy. *Written Communication, 12*(1), 4–46.

Dyson, A. H. (1997). *Writing superheroes: Contemporary childhood, popular culture, and classroom literacy.* New York: Teachers College Press.

Elbow, P. (1973). *Writing without teachers.* London: Oxford University Press.

Ellsworth, E. (1989). Why doesn't this feel empowering? Working through the repressive myths of critical pedagogy. *Harvard Educational Review, 59*(3), 297–324.

Emerson, C. (1986). The outer word and inner speech: Bakhtin, Vygotsky, and the internalization of language. In G. S. Morson (Ed.), *Bakhtin: Essays and dialogues on his work* (pp. 21–40). Chicago: University of Chicago Press.

Enciso, P. (1992). Creating the story world: A case study of a young reader's engagement strategies and stances. In J. Many & C. Cox (Eds.), *Reader stance and literary understanding: Exploring the theories, research, and practice* (pp. 75–102). Norwood, NJ: Ablex.

Enciso, P. (1996). Why engagement in reading matters to Molly. *Reading & Writing Quarterly, 12,* 171–194.

Erickson, F., & Shultz, J. (1992). Student's experience of the curriculum. In P. Jackson (Ed.), *Handbook of research on curriculum* (pp. 465–485). New York: Macmillan.

Field, J., & Jardine, D. (1994). "Bad examples" as interpretive opportunities: On the need for whole language to own its shadow. *Language Arts, 71,* 258–263.

Fish, S. (1995). Rhetoric. In F. Lentricchia & T. McLaughlin (Eds.), *Critical terms for literary study* (2nd ed.; pp. 203–222). Chicago: University of Chicago Press.

Flax, J. (1990). *Thinking fragments: Psychoanalysis, feminism and postmodernism in the contemporary West.* Berkeley, CA: University of California Press.

Florio-Ruane, S. (1991). Instructional conversations in learning to write and learning to teach. In L. Idol & B. Jones (Eds.), *Educational values and cognitive instruction: Implications for reform* (pp. 365–386). New York: Erlbaum.

Foucault, M. (1977). *Discipline and punish.* New York: Pantheon.

Foucault, M. (1984). *The Foucault reader* (P. Rabinow, Ed.). New York: Pantheon.

Freire, P. (1970). *Pedagogy of the oppressed.* New York: Continuum.

Freire, P. (1985). *The politics of education: Culture, power and liberation.* South Hadley, MA: Bergin and Garvey.

Gardiner, M. (1992). *The dialogics of critique: M. M. Bakhtin and the theory of ideology.* London/New York: Routledge.

Garrison, J. (1995). Deweyan prophetic pragmatism, poetry, and the education of eros. *American Journal of Education, 103,* 406–431.

Garrison, J. (1997). *Dewey and eros: Wisdom and desire in the art of teaching.* New York: Teachers College Press.

Gilbert, P. (1989a). Student text as pedagogical text. In S. deCastell, A. Luke, & C. Luke (Eds.), *Language, authority and criticism: Readings on the school textbook* (pp. 195–202). London: Falmer Press.

Gilbert, P. (1989b). *Schooling, writing and deconstruction: From voice to text in the classroom.* London: Routledge & Kegan Paul.

Gilbert, P. (1994). Authorizing disadvantage: Authorship and creativity in the language classroom. In B. Stierer & J. Maybin (Eds.), *Language, literacy and learning in educational practice* (pp. 258–276). Clevedon, England: Multilingual Matters.

Gilyard, K. (1991). *Voices of the self: A study of language competence.* Detroit: Wayne State University Press.

Giroux, H. (1986). Radical pedagogy and the politics of student voice. *Interchange*, *17*(1), 48–69.

Giroux, H. (1987). Critical literacy and student empowerment: Donald Graves' approach to literacy. *Language Arts*, *64*(2), 175–181.

Giroux, H. (1988). Literacy and the pedagogy of voice and political empowerment. *Educational Theory*, *38*(1), 61–75.

Giroux, H. (1991). Cultural politics, reading formations, and the role of teachers as public intellectuals. In S. Aronowitz & H. Giroux, *Postmodern education: Politics, culture, & social criticism* (pp. 87–113). Minneapolis: University of Minnesota Press.

Giroux, H., & McLaren, P. (1986). Teacher education and the politics of engagement: The case for democratic schooling. *Harvard Educational Review*, *56*(3), 213–238.

Giroux, H., & McLaren, P. (Eds.). (1989). *Critical pedagogy, the state, and cultural struggle*. Albany, NY: SUNY Press.

Goethe, J. W. (1970). *Italian journey*. London: Penguin.

Graves, D. (1983). *Writing: Teachers and children at work*. Portsmouth, NH: Heinemann.

Graves, D. (1994). *A fresh look at writing*. Portsmouth, NH: Heinemann.

Graves, D., & Hansen, J. (1983). The author's chair. *Language Arts*, *60*(2), 176–183.

Grimm, J., & Grimm, W. (1883). *Household stories* (L. Crane, Trans.). New York: R. Worthington.

Grumet, M. (1988). *Bitter milk: Women and teaching*. Amherst: University of Massachusetts Press.

Grumet, M. (1990). On daffodils that come before the swallow dares. In E. Eisner & A. Peshkin (Eds.), *Qualitative inquiry in education: The continuing debate* (pp. 101–120). New York: Teachers College Press.

Harris, J. (1987). The plural text / the plural self: Roland Barthes and William Coles. *College English*, *49*(2), 158–170.

Harris, J. (1989). The idea of community in the study of writing. *College Composition and Communication*, *40*(1), 11–22.

Heath, S. B. (1983). *Ways with words: Language, life, and work in communities and classrooms*. Cambridge: Cambridge University Press.

Heilbrun, C. B. (1988). *Writing a woman's life*. New York: Ballantine.

Henry, A. (1996). Five black women teachers critique child-centered pedagogy: Possibilities and limitations of oppositional standpoints. *Curriculum Inquiry*, *26*, 363–384.

Henry, A. (1998). *Taking back control: African Canadian women teachers' lives and practice*. Albany, NY: SUNY Press.

Hogan, D. (1990). Modes of discipline: Affective individualism and pedagogical reform in New England, 1820–1850. *American Journal of Education*, *99*, 1–56.

Holquist, M. (1990). *Dialogism: Bakhtin and his world*. London/New York: Routledge.

hooks, b. (1989). *Talking back: Thinking feminist — thinking black*. Boston: South End Press.

hooks, b. (1994). *Teaching to transgress: Education as the practice of freedom.* New York: Routledge.

Hymes, D. (1972). On communicative competence. In J. B. Pride & J. Holmes (Eds.), *Sociolinguistics: Selected readings* (pp. 269–293). Baltimore, MD: Penguin.

Jackson, P. (1968). *Life in classrooms.* New York: Holt, Rinehart & Winston.

Jaggar, A. (1989). Love and knowledge: Emotion in feminist epistemology. In A. Jaggar & S. Bordo (Eds.), *Gender/body/knowledge: Feminist reconstructions of being and knowing* (pp. 145–171). New Brunswick, NJ: Rutgers University Press.

Johnson, J. W. (1928/1992). The dilemma of the Negro author. In G. Early (Ed.), *Speech and power: The African-American essay and its cultural content from polemics to pulpit* (pp. 92–97). Hopewell, NJ: Ecco.

Johnson, M. (1993). *Moral imagination: Implications of cognitive science for ethics.* Chicago: University of Chicago Press.

Joyce, J. (1976). *A portrait of the artist as a young man.* New York: Penguin. (Original work published 1916)

Kamberelis, G., & Scott, K. D. (1992). Other people's voices: The coarticulation of texts and subjectivities. *Linguistics and Education, 4,* 359–403.

Kamler, B. (1994). Lessons about language and gender. *The Australian Journal of Language and Literacy, 17*(2), 129–138.

LaCapra, D. (1983). *Rethinking intellectual history: Texts, contexts, language.* Ithaca, NY: Cornell University Press.

Lee, A. (1993). Whose geography? A feminist-poststructuralist critique of systemic 'genre'-based accounts of literacy and curriculum. *Social Semiotics, 3*(1), 131–156.

Lee, C. (1993). *Signifying as a scaffold for literary interpretation: The pedagogical implications of an African American discourse genre.* Urbana, IL: National Council of Teachers of English.

Lensmire, T. (1993). Following the child, socioanalysis and threats to community: Teacher response to children's texts. *Curriculum Inquiry, 23*(3), 265–299.

Lensmire, T. (1994). *When children write: Critical re-visions of the writing workshop.* New York: Teachers College Press.

Lensmire, T., & Beals, D. (1994). Appropriating others' words: Traces of literature and peer culture in a third grader's writing. *Language in Society, 23*(3), 411–426.

Lensmire, T., & Price, J. (1998). (Com)Promising pleasures, (Im)Mutable masculinities. *Language Arts, 76*(2), 130–134.

Lewis, M. (1993). *Without a word: Teaching beyond women's silence.* New York/London: Routledge.

Lewis, M., & Simon, R. (1986). A discourse not intended for her: Teaching and learning within patriarchy. *Harvard Educational Review, 56*(4), 457–472.

Lofty, J. (1992). *Time to write: The influence of time and culture on learning to write.* Albany, NY: SUNY Press.

Marx, K. (1978). *The Marx-Engels Reader* (R. Tucker, Ed.). New York/London: Norton. (Original work published 1867)

McCarthey, S. (1994). Opportunities and risks of writing from personal experiences. *Language Arts, 71*(3), 182–191.

McDermott, R. (1988). Inarticulateness. In D. Tannen (Ed.), *Linguistics in context: Connecting observation and understanding* (pp. 37–67). Norwood, NJ: Ablex.

McLaren, P. (1994). *Life in schools: An introduction to critical pedagogy in the foundations of education* (2nd ed.). New York: Longman.

Michaels, S. (1981). "Sharing time": Children's narrative styles and differential access to literacy. *Language in Society, 10*, 423–442.

Miller, J. H. (1995). Narrative. In F. Lentricchia & T. McLaughlin (Eds.), *Critical terms for literary study* (2nd ed.; pp. 66–79). Chicago: University of Chicago Press.

Moll, L., Amanti, C., Neff, D., & Gonzalez, N. (1992). Funds of knowledge for teaching: Using a qualitative approach to connect homes and classrooms. *Theory Into Practice, 31*, 132–141.

Morrison, T. (1992). *Playing in the dark: Whiteness and the literary imagination.* Cambridge: Harvard University Press.

Morson, G. S., & Emerson, C. (1990). *Mikhail Bakhtin: Creation of a prosaics.* Stanford, CA: Stanford University Press.

Murphy, A. (1989). Transference and resistance in the basic writing classroom: Problematics and praxis. *College Composition and Communication, 40*, 175–187.

Murray, D. (1979). The listening eye: Reflections on the writing conference. *College English, 41*(1), 13–18.

Murray, D. (1985). *A writer teaches writing.* Boston: Houghton Mifflin.

Oates, J. C. (1990). *Because it is bitter, and because it is my heart.* New York: Dutton.

Oates, J. C. (1994). *Foxfire: Confessions of a girl gang.* New York: Plume.

O'Connor, T. (1989). Cultural voice and strategies for multicultural education. *Journal of Education, 171*(2), 57–74.

Power, B. (1995). Bearing walls and writing workshops. *Language Arts, 72*, 482–488.

Richardson, P. (1991). Language as personal resource and as social construct: Competing views of literacy pedagogy in Australia. *Educational Review, 43*(2), 171–189.

Scholes, R. E. (1985). *Textual power: Literary theory and the teaching of English.* New Haven, CT: Yale University Press.

Simon, R. (1987). Empowerment as a pedagogy of possibility. *Language Arts, 64*(4), 370–381.

Soliday, M. (1994). Translating self and difference through literacy narratives. *College English, 56*(5), 511–526.

Stallybrass, P., & White, A. (1986). *The politics and poetics of transgression.* Ithaca, NY: Cornell University Press.

Staten, H. (1984). *Wittenstein and Derrida.* Lincoln: University of Nebraska Press.

Taylor, C. (1994). The politics of recognition. In A. Gutman (Ed.), *Multiculturalism: Examining the politics of recognition* (pp. 25–73). Princeton, NJ: Princeton University Press.

Thoreau, H. (1960). *Walden.* New York: New American Library. (Original work published 1854)

Thorne, B. (1986). Girls and boys together . . . but mostly apart: Gender arrangements in elementary schools. In W. Hartup & Z. Rubin (Eds.), *Relationships and development* (pp. 167–184). Hillsdale, NJ: Erlbaum.

Threadgold, T. (1988). The genre debate. *Southern Review, 21,* 315–330.

Toulmin, S. (1990). *Cosmopolis: The hidden agenda of modernity.* New York: Free Press.

Ulichney, P., & Watson-Gageo, K. (1989). Interactions and authority: The dominant interpretative framework in writing conferences. *Discourse Processes, 12,* 309–328.

Vonnegut, K. (1973). *Breakfast of champions.* New York: Dell.

Walkerdine, V. (1990). *Schoolgirl fictions.* London: Verso.

Weiler, K. (1988). *Women teaching for change: Gender, class & power.* New York: Bergin & Garvey.

Wertsch, J. (1991). *Voices of the mind: A sociocultural approach to mediated action.* Cambridge, MA: Harvard University Press.

West, C. (1989). *The American evasion of philosophy: A genealogy of pragmatism.* Madison, WI: University of Wisconsin Press.

Willinsky, J. (1986). *The romance of expression as art versus education.* Paper presented as part of Concordia University Faculty of Fine Arts Graduate Studio Lecture Series.

Willinsky, J. (1990). *The new literacy: Redefining reading and writing in the schools.* New York: Routledge.

Willinsky, J. (1995). Learning to write: Gender, genre, play, and fiction. In J. Gaskell & J. Willinsky (Eds.), *Gender in/forms curriculum: From enrichment to transformation* (pp. 246–261). Toronto/New York: OISE/Teachers College Press.

Willis, P. (1977). *Learning to labor.* Lexington, MA: Heath.

Yancey, K. B. (Ed.). (1994). *Voices on voice: Perspectives, definitions, inquiry.* Urbana, IL: NCTE.

Index

About the Author

Timothy J. Lensmire is associate professor of education at Washington University in St. Louis, where he teaches courses on literacy and the politics and philosophy of education. His research and writing focus on the possibilities and problems of progressive and radical approaches to education.